The Henka Effect

How Coaching is Transforming Leadership and Organisations

Rachel Treece

The Henka Effect © Rachel Treece (2022)

PRAISE FOR THE HENKA EFFECT

This is the future of leadership! Offering a holistic and grounded approach, The Henka Effect is a fresh perspective that will help leaders transform their teams and organizations in the most critical ways to survive a fast-changing world."

Dr Marshall Goldsmith is the Thinkers50 #1 Executive Coach and New York Times bestselling author of The Earned Life, Triggers, and What Got You Here Won't Get You There.

If leaders are to transcend the moment and truly elevate themselves and their organizations, then they must learn to lead from both their heart and their mind. This book guides you through this elevated form of leadership with stories, interviews and insights that illuminate the interconnectedness between internal wisdom and external results. It demonstrates a better way to lead, a way that is inclusive, conscious, caring, and courageous, leadership that has the power to positively transform companies with lasting results.

**Dr Mike Watson
Spiritual Intelligence Expert**

In the Henka Effect, Rachel Treece presents a refreshingly original approach to creating inclusive and empowering work cultures. She explores and vividly illustrates the "magic" of shifting from a "command and control" style of leadership to a coaching style of leadership, with a focus is on the "whole person" and the "whole organisation". You will want to revisit this book again and again to glean the rich insights and practical tips Rachel offers to transform your impact as a leader.

Yvonne O Reilly
Founder Avant Team Consult, Master Coach

Leadership is all about impact – without impact, there is no change. The Henka Effect book is a powerful reminder that change first starts with self, and the book then provides a lovely framework and powerful tools to drive organisation transformation, starting with self. A must-read for leaders seeking to transform themselves and their business for greater impact.

Steve Hamilton-Clark
Chief Coaching Officer – The Henka Institute

We have long since known the value of coaching. With this book, Rachel Treece brings the art and science of coaching to life with the Henka coaching methodology. A must-read for any leader who wishes to help their people and organization thrive through change.

Stephen "Shed" Shedletzky
Founder at Shed Inspires and author of "Speak Up Culture."

Good leaders lead from within... they are soul inspired. This inspiration becomes effective when both their heart and mind are congruent. Through stories, interviews and many practical insights, this book helps you to better understand just how to develop that congruency and be a leader who has a positive impact both in their team and their organisation. A leader that the future needs.

Ross Swan
Co-founder Soul Inspired Leadership

Times have changed. The 21st century differs from the 20th in many respects. Although many resist the notion, we are moving from a time when employees were a resource engaged for the execution of a value chain engineered by the executive. Today, the employee is a key contributor to the creation of value itself. We have to adapt to information overflow and learn to navigate our way through fact and counter-fact. To be competitive, we have to ensure that our front-line workers not only are able to detect customer sentiment and desires but also be able to communicate ideas up to decision-makers effectively and effortlessly. To benefit from the potential of diversity, we all have to prime our abilities to both say our meaning, but also to listen to what is being said. In the knowledge economy, coaching, the skill of listening and asking the right questions, is part of modern management. A coaching culture is the means by which we infuse the organisation with the reality of the age-old wisdom that "two heads are better than one". This book explores many of the facets of what it takes to be a good coach and, more importantly, what is required to make everyone in your organisation a value-creating colleague.

Anthony Smith Meyer
Author of "Unleashing the Potential of Diversity in Organisations: Governance of Inclusion in a Racialised World".

This is a book that speaks to and from the heart. It is no accident that it is dedicated to her husband, whose day-to-day work experience, as for most of us, will have rarely benefited from management with a Henka mindset and to her daughter for whom, we all hope, the future will be radically different. Rachel argues that organisations can no longer afford not to have genuinely holistic leadership styles. I have seen organisations think they are trying this and fail. Not only does this book help to explain why it shows the path forward. It almost makes me want to come out of retirement and join in!

Michael May
Retired Former Financial Services Leader

The Henka Effect will enlighten, challenge, and inspire you. Rachel Treece masterfully weaves together ancient wisdom, neuroscience, stories, interviews, and a change model to engage and captivate the reader. Rachel brings honor and perspective from such great minds, Da Dao De Jing and Heraclitus, to Brené Brown and Amy Edmondson. She gives permission for leaders and change agents to embrace intuition and spirit. This book literally made me want to jump out of my seat and get further immersed in the Henka model. Thanks, Rachel, for your contributions to this important work. You are a gift to the world.

Jeff Kaplan, PhD, MBA, MCC
Executive Coach and Leadership Consultant – Founder Leading with Heart

I have followed Rachel's work for quite a few years as she has delved into systems and psyches of the business world, answering the urgent calls for change and transformation. Through deep research, engagement with a broad range of teams and individuals, as well as an authentic journey in self-reflection (critical to the integrity of this work), she has laid out frameworks, analyses, and pathways.

This book provides the tools for both understanding the challenges as well as the obstacles for meaningful change – and concrete steps to progress.. It will take you on a journey from heart to head, logic and emotions, to arrive at a sense of hope and opportunity. Rachel provides a subtle shift from empowerment to agency that is the key to unlocking the potential of systemic change

Hedda Pahlson Moller
Impact Catalyst and CEO Tiime

In every way, The Henka Effect is ahead of its time. Rachel Treece has captured the essence of authentic and human leadership with heart while bringing to light the need for organisations to adopt a more holistic approach to leading and managing people. I highly recommend The Henka Effect — an essential read if you're seeking a book to broaden your perspective on workplace management.

Mark C. Crowley
Author, Lead From The Heart: Transformational Leadership For The 21st Century

First published in Great Britain in 2022
by Babysteps Publishing Limited
https://babystepspublishing.com
© Copyright Rachel Treece and The Henka Institute

All rights reserved. No part of this publication may be reproduced, stored in, or introduced into a retrieval system or transmitted in any form or by any means (electronic, mechanical, photocopying, recording or otherwise) without the prior written permission of the publisher.

The right of Rachel Treece to be identified as the author of this work has been asserted by them in accordance with the Copyright, Designs and Patents Act 1988.

This book is sold subject to the condition that it shall not, by way of trade or otherwise, be lent, resold, hired out, or otherwise circulated without the publisher's prior consent in any form of binding or cover other than that in which it is published and without a similar condition including this condition being imposed on the subsequent purchaser.
ISBN: 13- 9798362143985

- **PRAISE FOR THE HENKA EFFECT** 3
  - Foreword 17
  - Introduction 23
    - **SUSTAINABLE PERFORMANCE – LEADER AS COACH** 25
    - **QUANTUM THOUGHT** 27
    - **DISCOVERING HENKA** 29
    - **THE HENKA INSTITUTE™** 31
    - **WHO IS THIS BOOK FOR?** 37
- **CHAPTER 1** 39
  - Coaching and the Curious, Changing Complex Corporation 39
    - **SOLUTIONS-FOCUSED COACHING** 40
    - **WHOLE PERSON COACHING** 42
    - **INSIDE OUT THINKING OR THE INNER GAME** 45
    - **AN ORGANISATION IS LIKE A HUMAN SYSTEM** 51
    - **WE HAVE THREE BRAINS** 52
    - **COACHING TOWARDS CHANGE WITH HENKA** 58
    - **ORGANISATIONS HATE CHANGE TOO: OVERCOMING THE RESISTANCE HURDLE** 59
    - **BUILDING A COACHING CULTURE TO SUPPORT TRANSFORMATION IN ORGANISATIONS** 60
    - **THE FUTURE OF WORK** 63
- **CHAPTER 2** 73
  - Henka and the effect of quantum thinking 73
    - **QUANTUM THINKING** 75

THE DAO DE CHING AND LEADERSHIP............ 81
HENKA AS A SPRINGBOARD FORWARD............ 85
THE HENKAQ PARADIGM: BRINGING IT ALL TOGETHER... 88

CHAPTER 3 91
Leader as Coach –Sustainable Performance and Transformation.. 91

THE CURIOUS CASE OF JAMES AND BILL.......... 93
CASE STUDY - SMALL BUSINESS ACCOUNTING 96
LARGE ORGANISATION PERFORMANCE............ 97
HOW COACHING HELPS ORGANISATIONS TRANSFORM 100
COACHING SUPPORTS TRANSFORMATION IN ORGANISATIONS – A CONVERSATION WITH JENNA 101

CHAPTER 4 109
HeartQ -Empathy and Connection 109

LEADING WITH HEART AND THE WONDERFUL DR JEFF KAPLAN 114
LEADING WITH HEART – MARK C CROWLEY – WHY WE NEED MORE LOVE AT WORK 116
HEARTQ – HEART INTELLIGENCE AND HEARTMATH® 128
COMMUNICATING WITH HEART – THE CONVERSATION 131
HEARTQ COMPETENCIES - HENKA LISTENING 133
THE JAPANESE SYMBOL FOR LISTENING 135

- INCLUSION 139
- **CHAPTER 5** 141
  - HungerQ – Purpose, Passion and Belief 141
    - HUNGERQ – THE INTELLIGENCE OF PURPOSE, PASSION, AND BELIEF 142
    - COMMAND AND CONTROL 143
    - OR PURPOSE AND SERVICE 143
    - INDIVIDUAL BELIEFS AND BRUCE LIPTON 146
    - ORGANISATIONAL BELIEFS 147
    - LISTENING TO YOUR GUT - 148
    - EQ - EMOTIONAL INTELLIGENCE 154
    - THE POWER OF AWARENESS 155
    - PQ - POSITIVE INTELLIGENCE AND EMOTIONAL SELF REGULATION 156
    - PURPOSE, PASSION, AND BELIEF AS THE FOUNDATION OF CHANGE 158
- **CHAPTER 6** 169
  - HumanSpiritQ – Culture and Identity 169
    - THE POWER OF SOLUTIONS-FOCUSED HYPNOSIS 171
    - THE HENKA METHOD FOR CULTURAL TRANSFORMATION 173
    - HUMANSPIRITQ - SPIRITUAL INTELLIGENCE 176
    - HENKA IMPACT - IT'S ALL ABOUT ENERGY 185
- **CHAPTER 7** 189
  - HeadQ – Open and Energising 189

- TRUST, SAFETY AND ETHICS (AND A BIT OF THE AWESOME STEPHEN SHEDLETZKY) 190
- HEADQ – HEAD INTELLIGENCE 206
- SUSPENDING JUDGEMENT 206
- COACHING AND NEUROSCIENCE 212
- THE WORLD ACCORDING TO FREDERIC LALOUX 213
- AGENCY 219
- THE POWER OF SYSTEM 2 THINKING – SLOW DOWN TO SPEED UP 221
- THE POWER OF PERSPECTIVES 222
- FUTURE SHAPERS/ORGANISATIONAL INFLUENCERS 225
- HENKA LEADER AS COACH 226

CHAPTER 8 229
- HenkaQ –Mindset and Muscle 229
  - MUSCLE – THE CRITICAL IMPORTANCE OF CONSCIOUS PRACTICE 230
  - MOVEMENTS – THE HENKA CORE COMPETENCIES 232
  - HENKA MINDSET 233
- Conclusion 237
  - THE IMPORTANCE OF HENKA IN CHANGING TIMES 237

ACKNOWLEDGEMENTS 241
- About the Author 247
- Bibliography 251

For Keith and Evie

Foreword

A new future is on the horizon – one that's different from the world before. More turbulent, less predictable, more complex, less simple, more varied, less knowable. It doesn't help that our brains are hard-wired to dislike change, so we tend to avoid it. The last year has shown that the world is what The Economist describes as 'predictably unpredictable': fragile, unstable, and decaying at a faster rate, with 41 trillion dollars of enterprise value at risk from the forces of business, technology, geopolitical turmoil, and workforce disruption. Now, the only certainty is uncertainty. Leaders must manage the relentless twin demands of performing for today while transforming for tomorrow by focusing not just on business continuity but on the sustainable performance of humans. That starts with coaching.

If leaders consider 'the one thing, they could do differently today to help their people thrive through uncertainty,' where would you start? In my role as a visiting professor and founder of a management think tank, I constantly hear about 'disruption' and 'change' and sometimes wonder if we're missing an important point which is that transformations fail because we fail to transform our people. That's why I love Rachel Treece's new book T*he Henka Effect – How Coaching is Transforming Leadership and Organisations*. With economic headwinds and tech disruption an everyday reality, coaching is a scalable solution to embed what the late Peter Drucker called a 'spirit of performance' that empowers humans to solve the biggest problems in the Organisation, calling out blind spots that leaders are blind to and making trust leaps into the future. One of the clearest signs of a culture of coaching is reframing and rethinking your assumptions about what stays, what changes and what goes. This matters because the complexity of issues today is outstripping our human capacity to respond, causing a high cognitive and emotional tax (too much time spent on shallow work versus deep work).

Leaders who coach others get to ask perspective-shifting questions and help turn uncertainty into a tailwind for learning, growth and reimagination. When you think about it, everything starts as an act of imagination but to sustain vitality for the long-term requires reimagination which I define as the human force that can push through inertia to create a better reality. Without reimagination, leadership breaks down; Organisations die younger, people stop learning and cultures decay. Coaching at its heart is a human-led platform for activating the curiosity to learn, the courage to unlearn, the clarity to focus and the conviction to believe. The Japanese word Henka (変化) means perpetual change, courage and transcendence and takes its inspiration from nature. It's turning lead to gold, oil to water or a caterpillar to a butterfly. It's the essence of re-imagination. When the future arrives faster than ever before, will you watch the world change around you and cling to the past or be the one leading it?

I want to thank Rachel for a vitally important and wonderful call-to-action book. We can all learn to be better coaches, and as a result go big on courage, equity, and joy at work.

Terence Mauri
Founder, Hack Future Lab
London, UK

Reimagination is your North Star.

The Japanese word Henka (变化) means perpetual change, courage and transcendence and takes its inspiration from nature. It's turning lead to gold or a caterpillar to a butterfly. It's the essence of reimagination: the daily curiosity to learn and the Deliberate courage to unlearn.

Will you watch the world change around you or be the one igniting reimagination as a platform for bold pivots to the future?

*Terence Mauri – Terence Mauri
Founder, Hack Future Lab*

Introduction

I woke one morning to hear the following words:

'I can't do this anymore.'

My wonderful husband was suffering from burnout. Keith had put in long hours in tough international workplaces for years and was always upbeat and optimistic. What had prompted this to occur at this time?

That day became the start of my mission to understand how performance could be truly sustainable. What had caused this? What had happened to my husband at that moment, and how could it be prevented?

The dimensions I discovered as I explored this issue surprised me–dimensions which extended far beyond **sustainability** (while they included it) and even beyond **transformation**. Not only did I begin to see an integration of Eastern concepts with Western ideals on a global level, but on a very individual and practical level, a means of moving forward emerged, which involved what Roger Martin calls "a third best way." This kind of integrated thinking culminated in my discovering and then developing Henka, an approach which I can only describe as touching on the **transcendent**.

I was encouraged when, along the way, I discovered current theories and voices espousing the need for a new way of leading by removing the "either-or" way of thinking to a more synergistic way that is not only superior but that enriches the lives of everyone involved. Henka, as we'll see, considers organisations as organisms; it relates, for example, to quantum theory; it is mirrored by HeartMath® (The HeartMath Institute is a North American organisation that has developed reliable, scientifically validated tools that help people reduce and avoid stress while experiencing increased peace, satisfaction and self-security. Research at the HeartMath Institute shows that adding heart to our daily activities and connections produces measurable benefits to our own and others' well-being); it acknowledges the interdependency and interrelatedness of all things. It is this inside-out mindset that also allows people to transcend and merge their unique brilliance with the greater whole of the company. This brand of sustainability involves a display of respect not often seen in Organisations and creates an environment that allows for the unleashing of creativity. It is engagement that does not lead to burnout, particularly because it is aligned with the individual's own sense of transcendence.

But let's start at the beginning.

When I first immersed myself in the research, I unearthed an underlying element that helped explain what had happened to Keith and to so many others like him. All indications pointed to a toxic culture. Such a culture has evolved over time because of poor leadership. There was a "do-more-with-less" mentality, no safety nets, and a win-at-all-costs culture.

I became fascinated with understanding what exactly high performance is and, more importantly, what makes performance sustainable. (Again, I started with "sustainable" and got so much more.)

What I learned is that organisations need leaders who are coaches.

SUSTAINABLE PERFORMANCE – LEADER AS COACH

In the 1970s, Nobel Laureate economist Milton Friedman popularised shareholder primacy or the idea that a corporation's sole responsibility is to increase shareholder profit. He claimed that executives work for the company's owners (shareholders) and that a company's only social responsibility is to "use its resources and engage in activities designed to increase profits so long as it stays within the rules of the game, that is, engages in open and free competition without deception or fraud." (Friedman, The Social Responsibility of Business is to Increase its Profits, 1970) The rules of the Friedman game have thankfully shifted dramatically, but some of this paradigm remains.

A high-performance culture is the foundation of this work environment. Global research firm, Gartner, defines a high-performance culture as 'a physical or virtual environment designed to make workers as effective as possible in supporting business goals and providing value.'

Studies show employees perform effectively in a high-performance culture because they are engaged, valued, and always learning. This provides work with more meaning, creating in them a mindset of continual development and a commitment to the organisation's objective, both of which drive performance.

As I learned from my husband's experience, toxic behaviours are one of the most serious risks to a high-performance culture or company culture in general.

'What a high-performance culture is not is cutthroat or destructive,' explains Catherine Tansey of Lattice (Lattice, 2021). 'Employee well-being, communication, trust, support, alignment of values, and a focus on development are all characteristics that contribute to a high-performance culture.'

You can have a dedicated team of driven, engaged, highly competent, and motivated high performers, but toxic conduct, whether it comes from senior management or other team members, will quickly turn a work atmosphere sour.

Toxic culture is one of the key elements contributing to what has been named the Great Resignation. High levels of stress are caused by low involvement or deliberate disengagement because of poisonous work culture.

QUANTUM THOUGHT

The great quantum scientist David Bohm once said, 'All the problems of the world are problems of thought. If we want to change the world, we need to change the way we think'. So how do we change the way we think?

Old (Newtonian) business thinking assumes that organisations are like machines which operate with certainty and predictability.

That way of thinking is no longer useful.

While classical Newtonian science views nature as simple physical systems that can be controlled and manipulated, in the quantum paradigm, nature is seen as complicated, chaotic, and uncertain. Weather and the human heartbeat are examples of chaos and complexity in nature. Quantum can be found everywhere around us. It's in our bodies and minds and practically every technological device upon which we've grown to rely.

Organisations are quantum too.

Uncertainty, which is integral to the Quantum model, calls for leaders to 'rewire' their brains and reinvent themselves to think and act in new ways. They need to become 'quantum leaders.'

A quantum leader is a leader as coach – a Henka Leader.

- A leader as coach can operate with uncertainty and instability, has a welcoming attitude towards it, and in face, flourishes in it.

- A leader as coach understands that 'the edge of chaos' is the finest place to foster creativity and innovation.
- A leader as coach brings to bear a wide variety of possibilities on a situation or problem and is willing to investigate them with the widest range of input from others.
- A leader as coach understands interconnected networks, conversation groups, and teams-within-teams
- A leader as coach creates teams that are given more leeway to take charge of their work structures and practises through self-organising. Agency.

Coaching as a leadership style helps to change the way we think. Coaching changes the way organisations think.

This book is about a quantum leadership coaching model called Henka.

DISCOVERING HENKA

So, what is Henka?

Henka– the Japanese term for *transformation* – is an evolving coaching methodology that supports the organisational transformation process in a **holistic** way. It makes transformation easier, lighter, and more effective. The result is improved and sustainable performance.

More about the word 'Henka.'

I've always loved Asia, and so, as my ideas developed, I looked to Asia for inspiration and became fascinated with the word Henka (変化). While Henka means change and transformation in Japanese, its more nuanced meaning is: 'having the power to make the invisible visible'.

Making the invisible visible is quantum thinking at its core. If we believe that a human being has three brains (mind, heart, and gut) in addition to a soul, *and* we acknowledge that an organisation is a system that contains human beings, then it stands to reason that leadership has to be quantum too. The bottom line of leading in this manner is a paradigm that is at once deeply complex yet beautifully simple. As with individual growth, so too with organisational growth. Henka is also beautifully simple and yet deep, rich, and complex ("like good Burgundy," my husband would say). The practice of Henka leads to mastery in the realm of leadership.

THE HENKA INSTITUTE™

Like any good Quantum entity, The Henka Institute™ emerged from the invisible to the visible with a change of focus. In this case, it was the result of some incredibly powerful coaching (in 2018 in Turkey) and a very relaxing holiday (amazing what the brain is capable of when it has a proper rest!)

That experience unearthed new possibilities, and I left Turkey primed for the next frontier in coaching. This is what I found:

Firstly, with the surge of automation comes the necessity for leaders to be increasingly networked systems thinkers. The increased complexity of work calls for more attention to be given to the interdependencies of all components. There has to be a vision of pulling it all together.

Secondly, it became clear to me that affirming the workplace as a human-centric entity is essential. That perspective, as we'll see, appears to be the next evolution.

This isn't about moving around already existing pieces of retraining leaders from one framework to another. This is about leaders, the great ones, taking their thinking to a new level. They themselves need to transform. And for this, they need transformational coaching.

We had already been implementing The Henka Method™ in organisations undergoing Mergers and Acquisitions, but it was my coaching session with Steve Hamilton-Clark which took our ideas to the next level. Steve is a former CEO and now an ICF PCC certified Executive Leadership and Mentor Coach focused on developing future fit leaders through his global coaching practice and is now the Chief Coaching Officer of The Henka Institute™.

Our vision was to help companies perform brilliantly <u>and</u> remain sustainable as they transformed. From my own experience with coaching, I suspected that it could be a contributing factor to this direction, but I grossly underestimated how powerful coaching could be in this domain.

In 2020, we launched certified coaching programmes designed to support organisations going through a transformation in an increasingly volatile, uncertain, complex, and ambiguous environment.

The Henka Institute™ aims to enable organisations to make a fundamental shift from command-control hierarchies to adopting a new cultivate-collaborate philosophy. It accomplishes this by superimposing a holistic influence on the entire coaching process: The **head**, with its influencing energy and potential for output of positivity; the communicating and connecting power of the **heart**; recognizing (and even evincing more) **hunger**–the seat of purpose, passion, and belief; and celebrating the **human spirit** through honouring culture and identity-- all amalgamate to create a quantum centre. That power centre is the HenkaQ, or where **Leader as coach** emerges. Think of it as accessing the Qi of Chinese medicine to enhance the whole system.

HenkaQ unleashes the broad range of human capacities into the coaching dynamic and this trickles into every corner of a company for its betterment. How the Henka building blocks all hang together will be explained later, but for now, let's take a quick look at the model opposite to get a preview:

So, again, put simply, the components are:

The Henka Model™ - How to Achieve Sustainable Performance

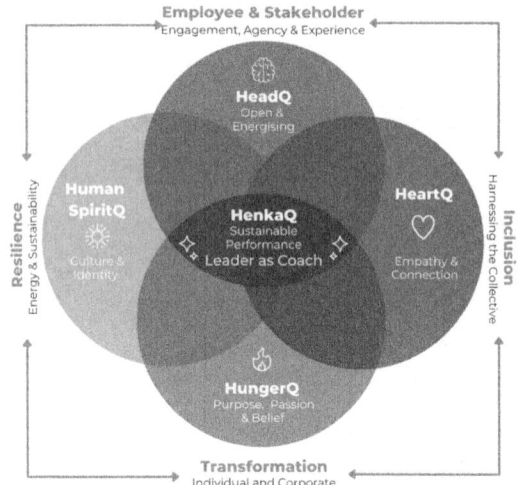

HeadQ – *Open and Energising* - This is all about being in a positive headspace/energy and suspending judgement, co-creating a path forward with others, supporting others in making trade-offs, and recognising cognitive biases and heuristics in self and others.

HeartQ – *Empathy and Connection* - This is all about creating a climate of trust and connection through listening, asking vs telling, and getting furiously curious for and with others. It's about seeing things from multiple perspectives, fostering inclusion, and inviting others' participation. People _feel_ seen and heard.

HungerQ – *Purpose, Passion, and Belief* - This is all about healthy emotional self-regulation (i.e., passion), having a clear sense of purpose, believing in others, being acutely aware of one's and others' strengths, persistently keeping the big picture in mind, and mindfully managing your energy, not merely your time.

HumanSpiritQ – *Culture and Identity* - This is all about having a deep respect for the human spirit, making values-driven decisions, having the courage and resilience to balance getting things done with developing people, and demonstrating compassion and wisdom.

HenkaQ - Bringing all the HenkaQs together, this is about having a deep desire to be furiously curious or passionately having the courage to ask questions for which you do not have the answer. Whatever comes up is used to support others in finding and executing their solutions in alignment with purpose. This includes belief in developing autonomy and creating a safe space at the deepest level possible, and connecting with the human being. This means holding off on judging or rejecting.

Rather it involves a willingness to be influenced in the pursuit of mastery for self and others.

Once synergy develops between all the interlocking and interfacing circles, the centre becomes both enriched and ready to spring forth outwardly again with its gifts. This is where Leader as Coach both nourishes and is nourished, and the quantum dynamic of the Henka Model can take effect. As is seen in the outer perimeter of the diagram, this dynamic radiates outward, creating winning experiences for all key stakeholders. Notice how they feed back into each other and how all parts relate to the whole in this holistic model. HenkaQ is all about leveraging the quantum power of a Leader as Coach to support transformation sustainably in self, then in teams, and then into organisations.

Henka™ was not invented in a day, a week or a year; it evolved. Henka™ is not static: it continues to evolve through the contribution of some incredible coaches, business minds and the Henkees™ (those trained in the methodology and who continually contribute to its meaning and evolution). And this openness to growth and interplay infuses Henka with its invigorating power.

WHO IS THIS BOOK FOR?

The times we live in are transformational, with the new replacing the old at a rate never before seen in history. That these changes are continually redefining the new normal is a "fait accompli", as the French say. Ideas that people used even five years ago no longer work. Martyn Cuff, the COO of Square Mile, told me, 'What people don't realise is that the pace of change will be exponential; we are in industrial era 4.0: the world won't be the same anymore.' Henka speaks to this kind of change.

This book is a book for ANYONE who has a significant transformation agenda, whether you are a senior leader, a transformation specialist, working in Human Resources or consulting inside organisations on positive transformation. This book is also for coaches who want to make a difference in their practice beyond coaching individuals and supporting organisations.

This is the book to help your development into a Leader as Coach. I believe that if we have more coach leaders in organisations, they will, by default, be more sustainable, employees will be more engaged, and clients will be happier.

I'm fascinated by what makes humans tick. I'm fascinated by what makes an organisation perform, grow, and be successful while the people involved thrive. I am fascinated by human tribes and the transformation in those tribes and what can truly support it.

I believe coaching is the key. I also believe that Henka is a uniquely effective key.

CHAPTER 1

Coaching and the Curious, Changing Complex Corporation

Coaching is a term that is bandied around a fair bit these days, isn't it? The Life Coach, the Executive Coach, the Sports Coach, the Career Coach, the Team Coach, and so the list goes on.

What exactly is coaching? Put simply; coaching is a process that aims to improve performance and focuses on the present rather than on the distant past or the future.

There are a huge number of coaching models, but I like to keep things simple, so I would categorise them into two major philosophies (though I am sure some purists might disagree with me here).

One is solutions-focused, and the other is whole-person coaching.

SOLUTIONS-FOCUSED COACHING

I like to think of solutions-focused coaching, metaphorically, as going to see your GP. You go into the surgery complaining of a headache, and you come out with a solution that will sort the headache out – some Ibuprofen, perhaps. You will take the Ibuprofen with some water, and the headache will disappear – that will be a great solution to the problem.

Solutions-focused coaching is a methodology that equips coaches with the means to help people effect change in their lives. It works through a partnership between coach and client and focuses on both the design and implementation of specific, meaningful changes in the client's personal and/or professional life. Solution-focused coaching moves the client towards a desired future outcome.

Fixing people's problems would be easy if the person were a car. You would check the engine find the cause of the trouble, replace the faulty part, and move on. People are not machines, however. Focusing on problems and their causes is a great way of getting cars back on the road, but it is not much use when you're trying to help people move forward.

I had an illuminating conversation with Martyn Cuff about the career of former Zimbabwean cricket coach Andy Flower, who was featured in the brilliant film, *The Edge*. (Douglas, 2019) Flower used performance coaching to achieve the most incredible results. *The Edge* reveals itself as a sensitive exploration of the effects of elite sports on mental health.

The film investigates the brutal intensity of the sport, the effects it may have on players' mental health and the high cost of success. The England test cricket team came from the bottom of the rankings between 2009 and 2013 to become the first and only English team since ICC records to be ranked number one in the world.

The team *was* transformed, and that was 100% clear. They obtained miraculous results that were also clear, yet the performance was not sustainable.

Flower himself said that if he could do it again, he would coach everyone as a whole person. He recognised that performance coaching was not sustainable. So, what is, exactly, whole, person coaching?

WHOLE PERSON COACHING

Whole-person coaching invites a different metaphor. I like to think of whole-person coaching as going to see the best alternative practitioner out there. The practitioner looks at you as a whole person, asks some penetrating, soul-searching questions and discovers that the source of the headache is…grief. The coaching has evoked awareness and an acknowledgement of grief. The coaching questions what you need to let go of. In letting go of the grief, the headache disappears.

The information you might find on whole-person coaching can make it more fluff than fact, in the same way, that you could perceive an alternative practitioner as a little bit too alternative. Whole-person coaching is anything but soft and fluffy. Delicate, maybe; inclusive of the intuitive, surely. It works to create positive, sustainable momentum for individuals, teams, and organisations. Put simply, the idea that we can separate our personal lives from our work lives or from our social or spiritual lives is nonsense. We are human beings

As human beings, when one part of our lives are disrupted, other parts are affected. Whole-person coaching not only addresses this but also integrates information from neuroscience and body awareness and considers the mental and emotional aspects of transformation.

When we started to develop the Henka philosophy, our premise was to focus on the whole person. Within the Henka Intelligence (HenkaQ) Model, we believe that a whole person, like a system, is made up of different parts. In various and evolving contributions, the whole person, the HenkaQ, incorporates the Head, the Heart, the Hunger, and the Human Spirit.

If you think of a person, we define them in terms of various perspectives: experience, intelligence, values, ethics, attitudes, maturity, skills, and education. None of these elements functions in isolation, and all the different parts form the whole person. And from the systems perspective, an impact, whether positive or negative, has a ripple effect on all the other components. A deficit in one creates an overall deficiency in the gestalt of the person in terms of both the evaluation of the individual and the coach's job of eliciting all his or her potential. This is one of the biggest challenges of a coach – to almost retain an aerial view of the person in terms of how the different parts work together to sustain the other.

In my experience, many leaders only focus on one or two parts of the human being. This approach, quite simply, does not deliver sustainable results. The leader will naturally then question the return on their investment in coaching and wonder why they should bother with it at all.

If you coach the whole person, however, engagement will be much higher, and with higher engagement, as we all know, comes better results.

With either philosophy, however, a great coach believes fundamentally that the individual always has the answer to their own problems and challenges but understands that they may need help to find that answer, which may include adopting lessons learned from other people's experiences – from the ancient world onwards. To be sure, rarely are people who are experiencing something unique (albeit unique from their worldview) the first to experience it (e.g. grief). There are philosophies, models approaches ...call it wisdom ... that people can choose to tap into and personalise to their needs to find their solution.

Henka is about

1. making organisations top-performing and yet sustainable during volatility, uncertainty, chaos, and ambiguity (VUCA)

2. helping organisations self-organise and creating a culture of agency through embracing a culture of Leader as Coach

3. supporting sustainable and optimum performance at "the edge of chaos."

INSIDE OUT THINKING OR THE INNER GAME

No introduction to coaching would be complete without mentioning the work of Timothy Gallwey and his book *The Inner Game of Tennis* (Gallwey, 1974) or the work of Michael Neill with *The Inside-Out Revolution* (Neill, 2013).

The Inner Game of Tennis revolutionized thinking about achieving success. Gallwey suggested that the key to doing this was internal, not external. His insight was that coaches could help individuals to improve their game by distracting them from their inner critic who said, "Not like that! Concentrate on your hands! Angle it differently!"

Gallwey saw that when the inner critic was diverted, the body could take over. It turns out that when internal dialogues are suppressed, the body often has a very clear idea of what to do. Gallwey used the example of asking people to focus on the height at which they hit the tennis ball. This activity has no relevance, but the simple act diverted the inner critic and enabled the capable body to take over. The individual relaxed, and their tennis improved immediately.

Gallwey's superb conclusion was that his findings didn't just apply to tennis but that individuals generally did have within themselves the answers to all sorts of their own problems.

At its core, coaching helps people to learn to silence that meddlesome voice and allow their instincts or inner wisdom, their subconscious, which allows a certain flow to take over. Sometimes that means distracting it, but sometimes it's about exploring the worst-case scenario and removing the fear.

The *Inside-Out Revolution* explores the three principles: mind, thought, and consciousness, that it claims are the source of our feelings. Since our feelings dictate how we experience the world, understanding what creates our feelings will mean that you can change the way you experience the world. This is a massive idea — and Neill explains it beautifully.

In a telephone conversation, I asked Michael Neill for his views on how coaching could help organisations transform. Starting with an overall perspective, he shared the following: "Just as coaching is the art of helping people get more out of themselves than they can get on their own, so too is coaching a profession designed for exactly what businesses want, which is getting the best out of their employees as well as to limit the damage they do when they're off their game. If you only brought in coaching for damage limitation, you would probably save a fortune, but if you could do both? Coaching, in its most literal sense, is essential to cost efficiencies. Beyond that, it is essential for all the connections that sustain cost efficiencies and effectiveness. And it is essential for well-being in the workplace."

I described to Michael what the Henka Institute is all about and asked him what he thought the impact is of having more leaders who can operate as coaches in corporations across the world. He points out that even if you're more of a leader as a servant than a do-what-I-say-or-get-fired leader, still, one of those things that people sometimes need is--*themselves.*

If people think that they can't do better, they can't have a better experience; they can't get along better unless the *company* changes, then you will have to go far to make that happen. But, if you are willing to get an in-depth understanding of coaching as a leader, you can show people that they can get what they want without the entire company having to revolve around their preferences. At the same time, it also gives you, as a leader, a much healthier view of your employees because instead of looking at them as people who can and people who can't, you start to see them as incredibly capable people that often don't know what's getting in the way of their capabilities and/or are just genuinely in the wrong job. And either of those can save you a fortune if you get onto it.

Michael appreciated the fact that besides well-being and cost savings, Henka was about *sustainable* performance for people and in organisations: "There's a lot of ways that aren't very "coachy" to get the most out of people. But it's not sustainable over time."

Knowing that Michael is not only about changing perspectives or thoughts but also about reaching beyond thinking, I wanted to know where he would go with the question that is really on my mind: "if one can change the thoughts of a person, can one change the thoughts or the beliefs of an organisation?"

He delivers by describing what he does as waking people up to what they're capable of beyond what they think, which includes their capacity for fresh thinking. It also bypasses the need to sort out their psychology or get bogged down in trying to have the 'right thinking', which is a kind of full-time job. When people start to see that, their thoughts change. There is a constant presence, and therefore, they don't get so bogged down in their moment-by-moment thinking or trapped in their moods.

Finally, I ask him—referring to one of his own quotes-- "how can corporations be awesomer?"

"The way the actual quote is worded," he corrects, "is 'Why aren't we awesomer?' and is intentionally phrased in this way. It almost turns the traditional question on its head as it sees 'awesomer' as the default. Said like this, we simply look for, "what is getting in the way of 'awesomeness' and 'amazingness'. We think that we are at the mercy of the economy. We think we're at the mercy of our boss, our colleagues, our work environment, and even our moods. Like this, we spend an incredible amount of time trying to control our conditions which is a very bad idea since it's very rare that we can do that in any lasting way."

Michael explains how we can give those things a nod while seeing our capacity as a constant. This, he says, changes your relationship with all those things. He illustrates this point with a charming story about his in-laws.

His mother-in-law was a city girl, and his father-in-law was a farmer. On the farm, she learned to drive the tractor. Eventually, they bought a car. After she drove it around, she went back to her husband and said, "I don't think we need the car, it's really no better than the tractor."

Surprised, her husband got in the car and had her drive around. "Well, why are you still in first gear?" he asked her. She said, "what do you mean?"

She just didn't understand how to get the most out of the car. The car was great. The car was awesomer. But she didn't experience it that way because she didn't understand how it worked.

That's what we're up against-- people have this extraordinary equipment that they don't really know how to use. A certain kind of coaching shows people how the equipment works. And once they get how the equipment works, they can do a lot. And it's already designed for that. We're designed for creativity; we're designed to thrive; we're designed to be resilient. We just don't know it.

AN ORGANISATION IS LIKE A HUMAN SYSTEM

I believe that an organisation is an organism or system like a human. To function optimally, it needs a brain, a voice, a gut, and a name, and it needs meaning. It also has conscious and subconscious aspects as well as beliefs. In fact, the words "corporate" and "corporation" originate from the Latin "corpus", meaning body, and the word "organisation" curiously has the word "organ" in it. Both are bodies that need care and nurturing.

A healthy and robust body is an indication of a strong immune system. It may need vaccines; it may need to develop muscle strength or become used to the certain motion, and it will certainly sometimes fail. Likewise, to thrive, a human being needs to practice physical health and put in place good habits for mental health, manage his environment, manage beliefs, be sociable, and connect with others.

WE HAVE THREE BRAINS

"In each moment of every day, a conversation is taking place inside us …. It's the silent, often subconscious, and never-ending conversation of emotion-based signals between our hearts and our brains, also known as the heart-brain connection." Gregg Braden -- (Braden, 2015)

I have sometimes wondered if the business world was entirely ready to hear about the work of Braden[1]. He can sometimes be billed as new age, but he is fundamentally a scientist. His books combine quantum science with teachings from ancient wisdom, and this combo seems to hold a key for bringing about some necessary shifts.

Braden argues that the heart has its own brand of intelligence, just like the brain. It is in reclaiming intuition and heart and bringing their status, at least, up to par with the intellect that seems to be invigorating modern work environments.

Coaching leadership responds equally to the Head, Heart, and guts (Hunger) of the whole team and trusts them to deliver outstanding performance. At Henka, we present later in this book that Hunger (read: passion) and Human Spirit are also critical components to the delivery of outstanding performance.

For example, one of the outstanding features of virtual environments is their demand for adaptation to rapid change. The assumption, then, is that a successful leader will help teams navigate those changes—with all the social and emotional factors that come along with change.

Another example is trust building. People are attracted to digital platforms that project trust. Trust must be developed within the team if it is going to be conveyed on a platform.

I also love the fact that Frederic LaLoux supports these ideas in his book *Reinventing Organisations* (LaLoux, 2014). LaLoux points out that today's belief system is rooted in a hierarchical worldview. In that case, there can only be one "brain" in command, one CEO for every company. But what we now know is that our gut and heart, which have become referred to as our "two other brains," are to be taken far more seriously than previously.

According to LaLoux, "[I]t might be no coincidence that we discovered or rediscovered the other two brains at the same time as the Internet became a dominant force in our lives. The Internet age has precipitated a new worldview that can contemplate the possibility of distributed intelligence instead of top-down hierarchy. With that worldview, we can accommodate the idea that we have more than one brain and that they can work together in shared intelligence."

This new VUCA (volatility, uncertainty, complexity, and ambiguity) world has a digital twist – the democratization of information through an ever more digitally connected world and labour force. This, combined with the concept that 'anything that can be distributed will be distributed' means that we're moving into an era of shared leadership … from 'I' to 'We'.

With the internet, anyone who has information has power – and historically, that's been churches and palaces … and now, it's us! It's your team members! The implication is that hierarchically led organisations are probably not the future. We're moving from an 'I' to 'We' business model where leaders simply don't and can't have all the answers.

Acknowledging the power of three brains in place of one calls for a reassessment of the description of CEO—and the possible realization that the notion of "boss" is becoming defunct. Organisations are learning to operate with a new paradigm—one that involves the CEO as a coach and one which involves more collaboration.

Whereas in the past, a hyper-focus on the technical might have upped production, the nature of today's productivity calls for a broader range of engagement. Technical expertise, while valued, no longer outstrips other elements, such as the emotional and social. And that calls for a manager who is savvy in bringing something that is greater than the sum of its parts. Much like a human being. Including the soul.

The effectiveness of approaching talented personnel with a synergistic attitude is outpacing the effectiveness of the command centre mindset. And this new way forward calls for a change in job descriptions. Job descriptions that don't evolve in tandem with constantly transforming work settings will result in people talking in two or more different languages in one company.

Remote work, due to Coronavirus, has only accelerated this evolution. Traditionally, a manager was someone who worked his way up through the ranks by mastering various tasks of the business. He then could train the next generation. Today, the next generation is more skilled and savvier with the workings of the digital world, so if there is a hierarchy, it could very well be reversed!

As technology continually encroaches on and even replaces this "graduation" process, a reordering of roles and a shift in dynamics is natural. Working with this new paradigm, "managers" are becoming most useful in attending to emotional and social dynamics and in promoting smooth networking between all the components of the organisation. In that capacity, the manager inspires, reflects, encouragingly questions, soothe, champions, listens, collaborates, and *coaches*.

We can get much further with the "3-brain" model, which acknowledges and integrates the mind with the heart and guts of the team. Yet, this coaching style of leadership is not used in organisations regularly, mainly because there is pressure from shareholders to get stuff done and get it done quickly. However, developing people takes time and energy. Much like a coach of sports, building a team that is cohesive, driven, and effective is often commensurate to the input of time and energy for advancing the overall team performance.

Joe Dispenza (Dispenza, 2019) talks about the three brains in a slightly different way; still, it is about synchronizing them. He explains that the frontal lobe is like the CEO of the brain and allows us to decide on an action to focus our concentration. The second brain, called the limbic brain, the emotional brain, is the seat of your autonomic nervous system. As you develop a skill or a habit,
You are beginning to synchronize the parts of the brain. You begin to master philosophy and act on it. When you do this properly, repeatedly, you activate that third brain called your cerebellum, where you really begin to develop and integrate. What emerges, Dispenza reports, is "a coherence as rhythm or order or synchronization. [W]hen the brain is incoherent, you're incoherent. And when the brain isn't working right, you're not working right."

And your company or organisation is not working right.

Synchronizing the parts of the brain brings us to a state of holism. As Dispenza says, "you go from particle to wave, from matter to energy, and you begin to liberate energy."

This unleashing of energy is what the coaching style delivers. This is the kind of transformation that creates huge benefits for individuals and organisations.

COACHING TOWARDS CHANGE WITH HENKA

"Leadership is not domination, but the art of persuading people to work toward a common goal." – Daniel *Goleman, Emotional Intelligence* (Goleman, Emotional Intelligence, 1995)

Why do most change management initiatives fail?
A whopping 70% of transformation efforts within companies are abandoned. Why? Research identifies employee resistance or management behaviour as the major barrier to success. This is not surprising when we get a glimpse into how the brain works.

Leaders are not equipped to support transformation
Martyn Cuff, who has managed many large-scale corporate transformations, explained that it is fundamentally due to human biology and psychology: He explained, "We are not meant to want to change. Change at its simplest level requires using energy, and biologically we are designed to conserve it."

hat is behind this phenomenon? More importantly, how do we meet this reality in an optimal way?

Daniel Goleman, a psychologist and science journalist, in his book *Emotional Intelligence* (which spent eighteen months on the *New York Times* bestseller list), discusses different styles of leadership, including the coaching style of leadership. He describes the coaching style of leadership as one that does not accomplish tasks and goals quickly but furthers long-term learning -- sustainability.

Goleman says, "people with well-developed emotional skills are also more likely to be content and effective in their lives, mastering the habits of mind that foster their own productivity; people who cannot marshal some control over their emotional life fight inner battles that sabotage their ability for focused work and clear thought."

ORGANISATIONS HATE CHANGE TOO: OVERCOMING THE RESISTANCE HURDLE

We absolutely need to understand how transformation occurs in human beings; otherwise, organisational transformation initiatives will either fail or waste money because the impact will be superficial.

If all life, including human life, has the instinct to conserve energy, then any change you make to a body at equilibrium will require additional energy to deliver the change. In other words, changes to a body at rest require extra work to achieve the change. As it is nature's instinct to conserve energy, it is also nature's instinct to avoid work unless the work involved (the expended energy) will incur an external source of energy, delivering an increase in energy to the discrete system.

For example, a house plant turning towards the sun decides to expend energy as it "knows" it will increase its discrete system's overall energy.

This is, of course, a vastly simplified illustration of the concept, but this can be applied to all forms of energy and hold true for every event in nature.

BUILDING A COACHING CULTURE TO SUPPORT TRANSFORMATION IN ORGANISATIONS

In 2018 the International Coach Federation (ICF) and the Human Capital Institute partnered to research coaching cultures in organisations. Some of their research findings (International Coach Federation and Human Capital Institute, 2018) included the following:

Coaching is one of the most useful ways to assist an organisation. In developing transformation management capabilities

A coaching culture can assist with building resilience, overcoming resistance, and developing change readiness
The use of coaching to lead creates an agile culture and gives greater confidence to employees who need to plan and execute transformation

Organisations with a stronger coaching culture are far more likely to have better talent and sustainable performance.
One-on-one and group coaching was by far the most helpful activity for contributing to the goals of the change management initiatives.

Among organisations that had a strong coaching culture, 61% were also classified as high performing. In contrast, of the organisations that did not have a strong coaching culture, only 27% were classed as high performing.

Magdalena Nowicka Mook, the president of the International Coach Federation, added some further thoughts in an article she wrote in 2019 (Mook, 2019). There, she characterises organisations that have a strong coaching culture as providing an environment where leaders listen actively and ask questions during tough conversations, which helps employees identify the barriers to progress.

Coaching is no longer seen as the preserve of senior executives, and organisations are seemingly on the verge of starting to understand that coaching is critical. These organisations have future shapers developing an environment that is creative and innovative and can be positioned for sustainable performance through transformation.

A Coaching Leader Drives Continuous Improvement

All organisations want to improve performance – fact. If they don't, they will perish. To this end, many embark on a major process of organisational transformation.

Henka Leader as Coach recognises the definition of performance as efficiency and profit but also knows that purpose, service, relationships, and values help to achieve that.

Organisations are beginning to recognise that to optimise performance improvement and behavioural change; their leaders must adopt a coaching style of leadership. Coaching is the leadership style of a transformed culture, and as leadership styles change from directing to coaching, the culture of the organisation will begin to change.

THE FUTURE OF WORK

I got curious about the future of work with all these changes that are happening to our planet, so I decided the best way was to talk to one of the planets leading experts on the future of work, the incredible Terence Mauri.

Rachel: Terence, what exactly do you think the future of work looks like?

Terence: It's a great question, and it's a question that we're all thinking about because everything changed - people changed, priorities changed, technology changed, the office changed. And the question we must ask ourselves is, 'Do we watch the world change around us, or will we be the ones driving that change?'

I say to people, 'Anybody that's been around over the last two years, you're already a futurist. Think about what you've been doing in terms of using all these different social media platforms: Zoom and MS Teams, and Hopin'.

I think the last two years… have been a moment of reflection, it's a moment of reframing, and we shouldn't waste that opportunity to harness the last two years as a tailwind for more accelerated learning growth and reimagination. And that starts with some great questions, so this first question that you've asked is an important one.

Now, what does the future look like? And I think an important message is that today is the slowest it will ever be in our lifetime. And depending on your personality type, that's either terrifying or exciting.

So how does that message make you feel?

Rachel: Very excited, very excited.

Terence: Yes, exactly. That's how we want to feel. So, you know things are only going to accelerate. This creates tremendous risk but also a tremendous opportunity, and we need to start thinking about three areas and three dimensions: the work, the workplace, and the workforce. So not just the nature of work, but why we work and how we work as well. And I think the point here is that what we're looking for now is more autonomy and more freedom over control, and this is a great opportunity to elevate and energize our why, our purpose, why we do what we do.

Rachel: I agree. So, we talked about the future of work itself. What's the future of leadership, or what's the future of great leadership? I'll put it like that.

Terence: Everything is being disrupted, so workforce models, technology, business models, everything's going off like yoghurt in the fridge. Most companies are still using leadership playbooks from the 1950s. Think about how much has changed in leadership, and the answer is not as much as we would like.

The truth is, I think most people are over-managed and under-led. What we need right now in this world is more leadership. So, I think there are several inflexion points that we are experiencing. We're moving from command and control, or hierarchy, to care and co-creation. We're moving from hierarchies to networks, from bossed to unbossed, from ego to eco.

And I think leadership is about we, not me. Leadership is not one person. It should be a team. In Africa, they call this Ubuntu. It means, 'I am because we are'.

Rachel: Oh, I love that! And I love that move from ego to eco. Love it. Fantastic.

Terence: For a real-world example, I spent some time partnering with Novartis. They're on a mission to reimagine healthcare, and as part of that transformation, one of their mantras is, 'Leading and embracing a perpetual state of beta'. That it's not just about transformation, it's about transcendence.

And I think this is where Henka—such a great word – comes in! Evolution. And what they're doing at Novartis in terms of leadership is moving towards unbossed, inspired, and empowered. And what that means is pushing down decision-making rights. It means we're moving the barriers to work, creating zero friction.

And it means going big on context, pace, and direction. I think it's about context over control now because the world is changing so fast.

Rachel: And what do you see as being the biggest mistakes that leaders are making?

Terence: There are so many out there. I saw one recently. It was a company based in California, and the CEO fired about 500 people in a Zoom call. This is one example, and I think what we're lacking is empathy; we're lacking compassion. We're lacking that human-led future. So, I think, as the saying goes, often leaders are blind to their own blindness, and so I think it's an opportunity as well, in terms of this future of work and future of leadership. If we want to scale futures that are more human-led, more intentionally diverse, more purpose-driven, and more we than me.

So, the biggest sins, I think, are narcissism... I mean, I once had a boss whose nickname was 'The Shadow'. He'd be working away, and suddenly, the air would go cold. You push it, and you feel a shiver down your spine, breathing like Darth Vader. And then a question, 'What are you doing, Terence?'

And the research is really interesting here because we can all relate to these bosses, and there are many different nicknames out there—the shadow, the interferer, the silent assassin, know-it-all, perfectionist, and we've all got our favourites.

There was a 10-year research study in Sweden looking at the effects of a bad boss. And the ratio of people who had heart attacks was three times higher when they had a bad boss. After family and life satisfaction, your direct relationship with your boss is the second most important factor in your overall wellbeing. It's that significant.

And the research I'm working on at Hack Future Lab shows that one in five people would trust a stranger more than their own boss. So, there's a lot of work that we need to do in this area because trust is the ultimate human currency. Money is the currency of the transaction; trust is the currency of leadership.

Rachel: And, Terence, if leaders are asking, "What's the shift I can make today to help me show up differently?' What would you say that shift needs to be?

Terence: It's a brilliant question. I think there are three big shifts for leaders to think about. Number one is who we are. What I mean by that is strengthening identity. It means purpose; it means culture, and it means a value agenda. When you've got a strong, operationalized, activated purpose—not just a company purpose, but an individual purpose. That's energizing. That you can connect with daily in a really deliberate way. You have more vitality, and it's a simplifier. It's a multiplier. It's a clarifier. It's an energizer.

Shift number one is to evaluate and energize and elevate who we are as a leader and as an Organisation. It means purpose, culture, and the value agenda.

Shift number two is how we operate and how we decide. We want to scale cultures where it's high quality and high velocity. Cultures that speak up rather than silence, cultures of courage over comfort. How do we decide?

How do we make decisions? It's an important shift and that means going big on decision rights, autonomy, freedom, and responsibility.

The final shift, and it's a big one, is how we grow. I think one of the paradoxes that leaders face today is performing for today while transforming for tomorrow. And that creates a real, very restless, a real paradox of demands on our attention. Because leadership is about attention. We're suffering burnout, and we're suffering overload, overwhelm, and anticipatory anxiety about the future.

So, shift #3 is how we are going to grow. How are we going to scale a sustainable and healthy ecosystem? Heightened wellbeing? And an Organisation that doesn't just focus on profit maximization but also human maximization.

Rachel: Absolutely. And coaching leadership style. How important do you think a coaching leadership style would be to support sustainable performance? I'm passionate about performance, but creating sustainable performance?

Terence: I think coaching is a superpower. Coaching is an incredible way to identify blind spots that people are blind to. Coaches can also ask questions that haven't been asked. Questions that can move us into different ways of thinking, different ways of leading and can remove barriers to performance as well.

So, I believe that coaching has entered the centre stage, and every conversation can be a coaching conversation. A conversation with some great outcomes that shift behaviours.

I did some interesting work recently with the leadership team of Pfizer. As we know, Pfizer had this moon shot of scaling a vaccine within 12 months or less. What they're doing at Pfizer is, they call them lightning-speed behaviours— back to the speed of science, crush bureaucracy, elevate purpose and trust, and make every conversation a coaching conversation where we play to strengths, we flag blind spots, and we really energize ourselves for the road ahead.

And that, for me, that's really inspirational. So, I think coaching is an incredibly powerful tool, a catalyst for more energy and more performance.

Rachel: And the last question. If you were to give one message to all our readers, what would be the bottom line here?

Terence: There are a couple of key points here. It's no longer business as usual. Business models and leadership models are dying, and you simply can't navigate a new world with an old map.

Terence ratified my own thoughts. A paradigm has most certainly arrived.

CHAPTER 2

Henka and the effect of quantum thinking

First, let us agree on what a paradigm is.

Thomas Kuhn popularised the concept of "paradigm" in his 1962 book *The Structure of Scientific Revolutions* (Kuhn, 1962). Kuhn argued that paradigms are like overarching theories that guide specific areas of science. A paradigm is essentially a particular view of the world.

Paradigm shift

The changing treatment for stomach ulcers is a good example of a paradigm shift. In the 1960s and 1970's my great-uncle, Mick, suffered intolerably from stomach ulcers. His pain and suffering were put down to stress, causing the secretion of acid that created the painful condition.

The medical recommendation was that Mick either needed an operation or life-long medication to reduce the acid secreted by the stomach. In 1983, however, the true cause of this condition was discovered: it is now almost universally accepted that *Helicobacter pylori* are the cause of most stomach ulcers, which antibiotics can cure. The medical fraternity at the time was massively sceptical –its members were in a different paradigm. The 1983 discovery marked a paradigm shift in medical practice.

Paradigms emerge to provide a framework for understanding phenomena (rather like a religion, in some ways). A paradigm gains acceptance if the community of interested scientists agrees that it fits with most of the observable data.

Paradigms are effectively one category of 'ideas' that sometimes, as in the above example, are very difficult to reconsider.

Another living paradigm is our current view on physics and connectedness. The current worldview subscribed to by most scientists is the theory of Newtonian physics. Despite ground-breaking experiments like the Geneva X in which Nicolas Gisin proved that particles behave in a connected manner even when they are miles apart, and the work of a Chinese institution that proved the effectiveness of healing through feeling and deliberate thought, and the output of 20th-century legends like Einstein and Wheeler, the Newtonian paradigm remains.

Leadership is also stuck in a paradigm that was created by Frederick Winslow Taylor in the 1890s. (Taylor, 1911)

The industrial revolution meant that companies grew far larger than ever before. Management is no longer involved in overseeing a few dozen employees directly. Huge corporations with thousands of employees evolved in this era. It's a key turning point in the history of management that led to many of the management theories that are continued to be used today. The paradigm remains as Newtonian Leadership. The current industrial revolution needs a new paradigm for leadership.

I want the impact of this book to be one of those that propel a quantum leap in the leadership paradigm.

QUANTUM THINKING

"Problems cannot be solved by the same way of thinking that created them."—Albert Einstein

So where is this new level of thinking to be found? I believe it has much to do with what can be called "quantum thinking." Whereas leadership in the past was more synonymous with commander, today, a coaching style of leadership is characterised by connection, cultivation, and collaboration. When leaders behave like coaches, command and control give way to collaboration and creativity. Blame gives way to feedback and learning, and external motivators are replaced by self-motivation.

Barriers fall, teams build, and change is no longer feared but welcomed. Short-term firefighting reactions are superseded by longer-term strategic thinking.

Instead of one brain driving the show, coaching leadership acknowledges the interrelatedness of the "three brains."

But this new way of thinking about leadership won't replace the old way without a more updated understanding of the dynamics that are in effect today.

Organisational systems mirror, or are an expression of, systems already in the universe. And there's no question that recognising that the world runs on a quantum paradigm has much to say about how we organise systems ourselves within that view.

The problems we are currently facing are not a result of technology or globalisation but rather a failure to maximise human potential. Humanity has never had so many options, yet we are not sure what to do with them. However, we are currently in what is known as the Information Age; many organisations still behave and think as though they are in the Industrial Age.

Stephen R Covey describes in his ground-breaking book. The 8th Habit how every change in civilization led to paradigm shifts in thinking. (Covey, 2004)

He states the need to alter the perspectives through which we see the world if we are to make quantum leaps and survive. He also talks about a "Whole-Person Paradigm", where he states we need to understand that individuals are full persons with a mind, body, heart, and soul rather than "objects" that may be driven and controlled. His eighth habit, which adds a third dimension to the other seven to help people progress from "efficiency" to "greatness," is about unleashing human potential by recognising the Whole-Person.

Eastern thought with Western ideals as a means of moving forward

This kind of thinking is supported by Roger Martin's idea of integrated thinking from a theoretical standpoint. (Martin, 2022)

According to Martin, integrated thinking aims to eliminate "either-or" alternatives and ways of thinking by guiding people to the "third best approach." A creative resolution of the tension in the shape of a new concept that incorporates components of conflicting ideas but is superior to each can be achieved by facing the tension of opposing ideas in a constructive manner as opposed to picking one at the expense of the other.

Too frequently, businesses concentrate on little problems and tick off boxes to "show progress," but nothing changes; instead, the problem is merely transferred. To genuinely transform an organisation, one must identify the leverage point at the heart of the problem, where resolving the issue will lead to a cascade of changes that result in long-lasting, beneficial change.

I mentally take a step back and ask myself what this means for coaches. Coaches are stuck in the paradigm, too. But that's where Henka can be a game-changer. And that's the unique world of Henka that I wish to bring the reader into. The Henka vision and method are for anyone facing a transformation challenge, for anyone who wants to be a leader that has impact and achieves sustainable performance. Its promise is to equip future shapers, quantum shapers in the coaching field, and for them to be able to impress a new overarching paradigm into organisations.

And HenkaQ is that quantum leader - leader as coach, with humanity, intuition, love, and compassion at its heart.

One such Quantum leader is international organisation consultant and executive coach Steve Marshall. Marshall draws on his experiences as a fighter pilot to deal with the onslaughts many companies face in the post-Covid reality. He describes pilots as having developed a heightened sense of their surroundings, something known as situational awareness (SA): "We paid fierce attention, noticing every detail of what was happening around us in fast-moving, complex air engagements. A keen, accurate sense of the "picture" was fundamental to our decision making and exponentially increased our effectiveness." (Marshall)

That quality of awareness necessary for tracking and responding to shifting tides is crucial for today's leaders.

At the same time, Marshall calls for breaking through facades, considering how best to serve the world and making a profound commitment to "Just being ourselves"[2] before making commitments in wider circles of influence.

What is becoming increasingly evident is that what was conceived for organisations yesterday will be considered myopic and outdated tomorrow. Proper surveillance or situational awareness (SA) in the cockpit of a fighter jet is imperative. The same goes for leaders of today's organisations. And as part of that, self-surveillance becomes important as well.

This, in fact, serves as a wonderful analogue for the Henka Effect. In the Henka model, the centre radiates out to the outer ring, and in the opposite direction, situational surveillance is conducted with resilience and in the spirit of inclusion. In other words, the company's core values are in balance with the furthest outreaches of the organisation's model (and visa versa). This kind of synchronicity loops back into itself and energises the whole system. This is where sustainable performance transformation becomes possible.

To find the most effective ways leaders can receive real-time data and stay on top of situational awareness, I decided to look at history and the wisdom of what has gone before.

THE DAO DE CHING AND LEADERSHIP

Like anything in life, there is usually a forefather of the thought. The Beatles were inspired by Elvis Presley. Elvis Presley was inspired by Gospel and Black RandB. Rarely is thought truly "new."

In the Dao de Ching, a great classic book, Lao Tzu talks about hands-off leadership, going with the flow of the system, and not trying to control the system. Particularly today, uncertainty is the norm.

The Dao De Jing and its Applications to Modern Business Leadership

Despite being written almost 2,400 years ago, the Dao de Ching's timeless teachings continue to be a relevant and guiding lesson for today's modern business professionals. In this great classic text of 81 brief chapters, Lao Zu teaches us about self-awareness, hands-off leadership, and acceptance of failure – teachings that continue to be discussed by the academics and the thought leaders of today. I would like to highlight three of Lao Zu's timeless leadership lessons that you can apply in your everyday life.

Personal growth through self-awareness

"Knowing others is intelligence; knowing yourself is true wisdom. Mastering others is strength; mastering yourself is true power." – Dao De Jing, Poem 33

When we don't know ourselves, how do we expect others to follow? Understanding oneself, one's values, and one's key strengths and weaknesses are fundamental to leading an Organisation. By knowing ourselves, we become better leaders because it guides us to make better decisions, create trusting relationships, and ultimately lead our team members to do the same. According to Philippe Clarinval, self-aware leaders help "create and foster a culture that encourages and promotes trust, which translates into happy employees and happy customers." (Clarinval, 2021). Therefore, self-awareness is the core of self-improvement and personal growth.

Knowing the difference between when to lead and when to follow

"The Master doesn't talk; he acts. When his work is done, the people say, "Amazing: we did it, all by ourselves!" - Dao De Jing, Poem 17

One of the biggest misconceptions about organisational leadership is that those with authority are the only ones who should lead. While this organisational structure can help achieve goals faster, you forego the team's potential to create impact, innovate and achieve great things together. Great leaders empower their teams to capitalise on their unique strengths and take on leading roles within the team. Great leaders do this by modelling "followership" and giving team members the space to lead, according to Oregon State University Doctor of philosophy Hannah Gosnell. (Gosnell, 2020) Knowing when to lead and when to follow is both an art and a science. While it takes time and practice, when done harmoniously, it can create for the leader and yield extraordinary results for the team.

Accepting the unknown, even if it means failing

"True mastery can be gained by letting things go their own way. It can't be gained by interfering." - Dao De Jing, Poem 48

As human beings, it is natural to fear what we don't know. We desire to have complete control over our environments and avoid situations that risk the possibility of failure. When we stick to what is familiar, however, we deprive ourselves of learning opportunities that help us grow and become better individuals. Lao Tzu teaches us that we should allow things to progress naturally and learn to deal with issues as they arise, even if it leads to failure. These lessons help us grow so we can become better versions of ourselves and learn to show up every day with courage. It is only by accepting the unknown and allowing things to go their natural course that we develop the skills needed in a rapidly changing and dynamic society.

Putting it All Together

In conclusion, Lao Zu's *Dao De Jing* is as relevant today as it was many years ago. Its lessons continue to be acknowledged because of their applicability on our journey to be business leaders. Self-awareness, being able to distinguish between hands-on and hands-off leadership, and acceptance of the unknown are key lessons all business professionals should practise in order to become great leaders. Truly, Laozi's ancient text continues to reveal modern and profound leadership lessons for the everyday business professional.

HENKA AS A SPRINGBOARD FORWARD

Inherent in the Japanese word Henka (変化) for change and transformation is the implication of: 'having the **power to make the invisible visible**.'

Making the invisible visible is quantum thinking at its core. Just as the human self does not consist of a series of little boxes separately labelled 'mind,' 'heart,' 'spirit,' 'gut,' an organisation doesn't just consist of a series of smaller divisions which are separately labelled, 'product development,' 'marketing,' 'finance,' and so on.' Similarly, Frederick Taylor espoused a fragmented approach to change, one in which different parts are viewed as isolated, cubical-like, one from another. Taylor's model of the company as a machine was taken directly from Newton's work. The whole culture bought into this working perception of disjointedness. Coaching needs to springboard away from this model to meet the newest challenges for a company's growth.

But we agree that the brain works against new ideas; the brain itself is wired to strengthen what it already thinks. This is what a coach has got to work with.

This is also where Bruce Lipton's 'quantum' view becomes relevant.

Bruce Lipton wrote the compelling book, *The Biology of Belief*. (Lipton, 2016). Lipton's work relates to individuals and the human body, but if we believe that a corporation is also the representation of a body, then it stands to reason that many of his theories can also apply to organisations.

He tells us, "The brain is the chemist. You change the picture; you change the chemistry. Genes are not the metric [of the universe]—consciousness is."

In a view that is 180 degrees from the Newtonian vision of reality, he tells us that 7 billion humans come together to create a super-organism called humanity. In this paradigm, all are interrelated and relevant in the greater system. And this is particularly significant when we talk about the role of the subconscious and how we can change beliefs to enhance any system or organisation.

A lot must happen for organisations to keep pace with today's metamorphosing world. While organisations need to meet an ever-increasing client sophistication and meaningfully manage the complexity and volume of data, they need, at the same time, a belief system and mindset that can evolve and adapt and help the whole system thrive. Henka brings all the parts of the system into a unified unit where leaders are trained in proven coaching techniques, introducing all that enhances the health of the whole system. As Steven Covey, Roger Martin and Bruce Lipton make evident; a system thrives in a quantum way when it is seen as a living, breathing body. This is the power to make "the invisible visible" and energize every level of an organisation.

In a competitive world, leaders are under pressure to deliver value: to be innovative and visionary and demonstrate the right behaviours to move their organisation forward. For this to happen, embedding a coaching culture in organisations is essential.

This is the "Leader as Coach" which Henka seeks to facilitate and promote. Transformation can only really be achieved if it is embedded in organisations through future shapers who use the power of coaching to unveil new insights whilst maintaining the core values that make each business unique.

THE HENKAQ PARADIGM: BRINGING IT ALL TOGETHER

The HenkaQ Paradigm pulls these concepts together. HenkaQ stands for **H**enka **I**ntelligence and is an integrative and organic model that moves with change—even rapid change.

A person with strong HenkaQ easily accesses the Head (Mind), Heart, Hunger (Gut) and Human spirit (Soul) in a way that allows them to operate as leader as coach. While someone may have been born with some or many innate HenkaQ capabilities, studies show that, just like chess or martial art, to become proficient as a Henka master (Leader as Coach) requires regular and deliberate practice.

Once synergy develops between all the interlocking and interfacing circles, the centre becomes both enriched and ready to spring forth outwardly again with its gifts. This is where Leader as Coach both nourishes and is nourished, and the quantum dynamic of the Henka Model can take effect. As is seen in the outer perimeter of the diagram, this dynamic radiates outward, creating winning experiences for all key stakeholders. Notice how they feed back into each other and how all parts relate to the whole in this holistic model.

HenkaQ or Henka Intelligence, or the power to be Leader as Coach, is, therefore, the capability to support transformation sustainably. This is the masterful combination of all.

In his book, *Cracking Great Leaders*, Bruce Holland (Holland, 2015) believes that the understanding of this symbiotic relationship between Head, Heart, Body, and Soul enables leaders to see people as whole persons. Transformation through recognising that you deal with something bigger than just the obvious physical person creates what Bruce Holland refers to as "goose bump moments." Think of looking at organisations to find their soul. It is only through finding the soul of the organisation that we can attempt to change its physical realm.

This is the new paradigm for leadership.

In the next chapters, I want to explain how this new paradigm works.

CHAPTER 3

Leader as Coach – Sustainable Performance and Transformation

It is not the strongest that survive or the most intelligent, but the ones most responsive to change. --Charles Darwin

I was nine years old when my dad came home from work one day and said:

"I've lost my job".

With his second breath, he said

"I've packed in smoking."

My dad had been a smoker since I was born. I can always remember those Benson and Hedges gold packets lying around the house. He even dabbled in a little bit of pipe smoking in the 70s. Holding the edges of his moustache, he and a friend, Ernest, used to brew up beer in nappy boilers in the kitchen. It beggars belief! The stench of the beer, the cigarettes hanging out of their mouths, and Tom Selleck's looks will always stay with me.

He was as good as his word. He never smoked again. He knew that without a job, he wouldn't be able to maintain both a family and a nicotine habit, and thankfully, we were the priority. If he found it hard to give up, he certainly never let on.

From just what I have seen among my own circle of acquaintances, people seem to have widely varying appetites for change, depending on both their own personalities and how imperative the need is to change course.

Humans run organisations-- at least, I have not met one thus far that is not, and so, it is with the human character, resistance, and all that we must contend.

The following contrast of responses highlights how, in our humanness, we respond well or resist change, leading to vast differences in outcomes. How might one approach or the other impact an organisation?

THE CURIOUS CASE OF JAMES AND BILL

James had a heart attack back in 2006. He'd always been an intensively hard worker and had clocked up long nights working for an international bank. As soon as he returned to work following this life-changing episode, James decided things were going to be different. He made three big changes to his daily routine. 1. He was never going to drive into town anymore, opting instead for the train. 2. He would leave work at six p.m. on the dot, and 3. he would finally fit some exercise into his schedule. He carried through with all three changes. He was transformed.

By contrast, Bill had a heart bypass in November 2019. He was a heavy smoker and drinker, a bon viveur, a rock star. With cavalier disregard for the surgeon's counsel, he was back on the cigarettes and cocktails by New Year's Eve 2019.

In most cases, dramatic events can shake a person up enough to lead to personal transformation-- and often quite quickly. But it's not guaranteed. So why are human beings so resistant to change when they know that the status quo is doing them harm?

Research tells us that this is "normal" human behaviour. We, as human beings, are naturally scared of the new because we fear that the unknown may harm us. This cautious approach has, indeed, contributed to our survival, enabling our species to evolve and making it possible for me to write this book today. However, resistance to change does not serve us well in our global society in the 21st century. We are terrible at change, and change is exactly what is called for in our post-modern age!

And if we struggle with changing ourselves at an individual level, even when there are pressing reasons for us to do so, how much harder is it to bring about change at an organisational level when you are dealing with hundreds or even thousands of people, all with different motivations?

So, if we agree that the organisation that is most adaptable to change is the one that will survive, in terms of performance and sustainability, why is it so difficult for an organisation to change?

My presupposition involves the fact that an organisation is a collection of humans, and maybe one of them is James, but one is Bill, as in the above example. Let's make this even clearer: let's suppose for the moment that one is James, aged six, and one is Bill, aged six. Imagine I told Bill, "Hey Bill, you really shouldn't touch the fire!" or, "Bill, you really shouldn't have another sweet from the sweet drawer."

Bill, being Bill, got sick of following blindly. Why shouldn't he touch the fire? Why shouldn't he have another sweet from the sweet drawer? Bill didn't understand why he should or shouldn't do something, so he would kick up a fuss or rebel and do the opposite.

What does this mean for our organisations? I spoke to Robert McKillop, a senior asset management executive who has coached children and adults in rugby. He told me that if you coach a kid in rugby and want them to do something, and your language is unclear, they will tell you: "Huh? What d'ya mean?" Conversely, adults are far more reluctant to let on when they are not clear about an instruction.

Notice in the following account the value of having a leader with acute situational awareness (clarity) and healthy self-surveillance is imperative in navigating change.

CASE STUDY - SMALL BUSINESS ACCOUNTING

Roger and Jane ran a small service business and were keen to outsource the accounting for two reasons: 1) it brought resilience to their business - what if the CFO, John, got sick? He was the only one in charge of maintaining the financials; 2) they had no real oversight of their accounts because John was wedded to a complex desktop accounting system that they didn't understand, and reporting was rarely provided due to the time that it took to collate.

For eighteen months, Roger and Jane used a collaborative leadership style to get John to move the accounts onto a cloud-based system and liaise with a local accountant. It didn't work.

Frustrated, Roger and Jane took the challenge to the board, who concluded that the outsourcing had to happen. It still didn't. Even a board resolution was not enough to galvanise John into action. (He shared the same propensity - to stick with the familiar even to his own detriment (as Bill of the triple by-pass story).

Finally, after engaging in some coaching for themselves, Roger and Jane realised that they were being too tolerant, allowing themselves to march to John's tune, which was detrimental to what they wanted and not in the best interests of the company. They had no choice; they had to employ a more autocratic leadership style for this case. This was not their natural or preferred style, but it was necessary for pushing through their wishes. And push through they did. In retrospect, the cloud-based system was clearly the way to go, and now they have on-time, resilient and transparent financials.

What might they have achieved if they had adopted a coaching style earlier on in this journey?

LARGE ORGANISATION PERFORMANCE

Here, we get to what 'Optimal Performance' really means. Anita Baggio, at the time a co-leader at McKinsey in Latin America for culture and change work, in a 2019 article, talked about the Chief Transformation Officer of a consumer goods manufacturer who was under pressure to improve after not having performed well for several quarters. The Chief Transformation Officer went off to set more stretching targets and created a weekly set of KPIs (key performance indicators) to review performance initiatives with more rigour.

Initially, some KPIs improved, but soon it was obvious that the whole project drained more energy than could be justified by the incremental improvement in results. People were disengaged.

The article goes on to conclude that most organisational transformations focus on KPIs and only give a cursory glance at employee behaviours as an afterthought. In addition, they often forget the main reason they needed a transformation in the first place.

Another expert from McKinsey, Bill Schaninger, who designs and manages large-scale organisational transformations, adds: "Successfully transforming an organisation continues to be one of the greatest challenges facing leaders, as it requires changing the behaviours and underlying mindsets of a critical mass of people". He continues, "By personalising tried-and-true strategies, leaders can drive lasting change at scale". (Schaninger, 2020)

I asked Robert McKillop, one of the financial services industry's greatest leaders, about transformation. He said: "One of the main problems with transformations is that there is no clear articulation of what the lighthouse – the promised land - looks like. If you have no clear idea of what the promised land looks like, how on earth will you know when you get there?" Lack of a clear vision saps employees of motivation. Reaching a clear goal is its own reward; it is a natural source of satisfaction, and your employees will work to get there. The KPIs will rise with the tide.

Antoine de Saint-Exupery articulated this in another way

> "If you want to build a ship, don't drum up people to collect wood and don't assign them tasks and work, but rather teach them to long for the endless immensity of the sea." - Antoine de Saint-Exupery

Overnight: working from home

According to the great psychiatrist Viktor Frankl, "Every human being has the freedom to change at any instant." (Frankl, 1946) This is just as well, as sometimes resistance is swept away by the force of necessity. Consider the work-from-home issue:

Organisations had hard-working groups discussing the possibility of working from home for years. Hours were spent on the topic, with huffing and puffing (this is a phrase my mum uses for people who blow hot air and don't do a lot of work). There was no solution; the possibilities of working from home were limited. Then came covid-19, with its paradoxical dark and light shadows, and on the turn of a sixpence, everyone was working from home!

The transformation had happened. Literally overnight.

Coronavirus won't always be present, but the transformation will be. We have forgotten that we are consistently dealing with the complexities of human *beings*, not human *doings*.

HOW COACHING HELPS ORGANISATIONS TRANSFORM

In the corporate world, coaching was once exclusive to senior leaders in the form of executive coaching. More recently, it has become commonplace to help employees, managers and senior leaders improve their contribution to organisational success.

In addition, employee engagement and cultural change have truly started to become key initiatives for corporates, enabling coaching to play a key role in the organisational transformation process. Organisations know now that highly motivated employees produce excellent results, and some organisations even offer in-house cultural development programmes that include a coaching mindset, coaching leadership, and general coaching skills.

Even if you didn't believe it before, you could now see how our world is changing in front of our eyes. Leadership development has become ever more critical in organisations – not least with the need to think more about succession planning and ways to diversify. There is now an increased emphasis on the ability to interact with people. In summary, future shapers in organisations will have coaching as a key part of their development.

COACHING SUPPORTS TRANSFORMATION IN ORGANISATIONS – A CONVERSATION WITH JENNA

Fundamentally, I believe the following: Coaching is the means to sustain organisations and help them transform.

To find out more about **how** coaching supports the transformation agenda, I talked to Jenna Filipowski, PhD who was the former head of research at the Human

Capital Institute in the USA. In 2018, Jenna undertook a piece of research on the following topic:

What does it even mean to have a coaching culture?
And once you do have it, for which mechanisms?
And finally, what are the optimal ways to use it overall?

The research she conducted (ICF and Human Capital Institute (HCI), 2018) explores the concept of change management. Obviously, we all experience change continuously. But if you want to *manage* change, *plan* for change, and *help people through* change, you need to take control of it. Below, Jenna shares her thoughts on facilitating change using coaching principles.

Rachel: How can coaching be part of the transformation agenda?

Jenna: There are a variety of ways to bring a coaching culture into an organisation:

- You can have internal coaches trained in coaching methods for working with your people through change.
- You can provide coaching skills to your managers and leaders to help their teams through change.

- Peers and people on teams could use coaching skills to work with each other by encouraging questions around the change. This is instead of just telling people what to do and to "get over it."
- You can employ or contract external coaches to come in and set up a coaching program to work with your people as they ready themselves to go through the change.

Rachel: Do you have a view on which is the most successful of those two coaching approaches for companies: internal or external?

Jenna: It depends on the culture, on the budget, and on the size [of your organisation]. Sometimes, it is only a small group of people that needs to experience coaching. In that case, it might be more effective just to bring someone in from outside to work with that specific group of people for a defined period.

The research that we (HCI) produced with the International Coaching Federation showed that the greater number of modalities you must choose from, the better because you can reach people in a variety of ways. When coaching is embedded inside an organisation through an internal program--with managers and leaders using coaching skills--you can engage more fully in useful coaching. You can use outside coaches and external coaches for more targeted and specific needs. An example of this may be a conflict of interest that arises that can't be resolved internally.

Rachel: What sort of mindset shift, or paradigm shift, needs to happen for some organisations to embrace this? What is it that commonly blocks organisations?

Jenna: You cannot separate the need for a coaching culture from other issues and priorities within HR, such as management, leadership development and talent acquisition. Organisations must be committed to growth and change and have leaders who understand that organisational value lies in the talents of their people.

Coaching is seen as another tool in their toolkit. As with an onboarding program or employer branding efforts, they're all part of a suite of tools related to the value you place on your workforce and your confidence in HR professionals to get that work done.

Rachel: Why do you think coaching works so well? People change is hard, and behaviour change is even harder. You need support, encouragement, and feedback to make that happen. You can't just announce: "I'm going to be different today", without having reinforcement, without a testing and support system in place, or without someone to keep you accountable.

Jenna: Coaching can become a continuous part of every learning experience or intervention that you provide. It's not a "one-and-done" exercise of learning.

Rachel: Was there a "Wow!" moment that occurred while analysing your research?

Jenna: Yes, absolutely. When I interviewed change management practitioners for our research on the integration of change management and coaching, they would say, "Oh, why didn't I think about that before?"

It became apparent that **coaching** and **change management** were orbiting on two distinct planes. Professionals weren't inhabiting both worlds or integrating them. Hopefully, this research will change some thinking about change management as a discipline. There are people who are highly trained in those processes and programs, but without coaching, something profound and overarching is missing in the process, which impacts the health, vibrancy, and effectiveness of an organisation.

Rachel: It seems like it could almost be likened to a family unit (especially one that is about to undergo some kind of change): You can't just hand out tasks with an eye on productivity or desired outcome. There's more process, more humanity to it than that.
Have you seen shifts since then [2018 when the research was undertaken]?

Jenna: Coaching as a practice has become more prominent; people talk about it more. They're more interested in technologies for coaching and how to get coaching to more people more easily. More organisations are interested in leading with coaching in place of leading solely with training.

People who aren't in HR have more familiarity with what coaching is, which is great for the profession.

Change management and HR professionals can miss a crucial element about the building blocks of an organisation--that is, the individuals and principles that make it up. Viewing these "building blocks" through very human lenses is something that coaching can bring about and is a distinguishing factor in the Henka model. How an organisation facilitates change will test its sturdiness; therefore, attention needs to be given to the foundation and structure in a new way.

That new way is Heart.

CHAPTER 4

HeartQ – Empathy and Connection

It has been universally acknowledged throughout history that the heart is the source of love, wisdom, intuition, and courage.

"Put your heart into it," "learn it by heart," and "talk from your heart" are all phrases that everyone is familiar with. All imply an understanding that the heart is more than a physical pump that keeps life going. People have relied on their hearts – often known as their inner voice, soul, or higher force – for guidance throughout history.

There is much evidence that shows that the heart is infinitely wiser than the brain. According to Dr Kimble Green, author of *The Monarch Method*, 'The science of wisdom and where it originates goes back centuries. The beauty is you are far wiser and more brilliant than you know - it's all about heart!' (Greene, 2012)

The truth is your inspiration and wisdom come from your connection to your inner brilliance, including your HeartQ and HumanSpiritQ.

Figuring things out (using your head) is helpful when piecing together a puzzle, repairing a machine, or interpreting a map, as you will see in the HeadQ chapter. Feeling it out (using your Heart, Hunger, 6th sense, gut feeling, intuition, and Human Spirit) offers you the wisest answers and solutions for almost everything else. The human brain, your cognitive thinking abilities, and your physical senses — sight, sound, hearing, touch, and smell – are all built for survival in this physical environment and serve you well in that role.

How many times have you overheard someone say that their wonderful idea — a book, movie, structure, concept, or anything – came to them out of nowhere? That's because most discoveries and ideas don't come from simply thinking it out (*head) but from first feeling it out. Albert Einstein, one of history's most prolific physicists, is an excellent example. In his writings, he claims that his theories and ideas sprang from his mind. He screams, "Knowledge is less important than imagination. Because knowledge is restricted, whereas imagination encompasses the entire world, spurring growth and allowing evolution to occur."

In his 2019 blog for Human Capital Online about leading with heart, Richard Rekhy tells us that wise and true leaders are passionate about their dreams and goals, regularly live out their values, and lead with their hearts as well as their intellect. "A good head and a decent heart are always a strong combination."

They are aware of who they are on the inside as much as they are about who they are on the outside.

Rekhy continues to share a story about Nelson Mandela's inspiration. When he was elected President of South Africa, the country was divided. He believed that using sport to bring the country together was the finest idea. Mandela and then-South African rugby captain Francois Pienaar met just before the Rugby World Cup in 1995. "Dr Mandela merely spoke about leadership, etc., and while he did not say it, his eyes said that he wants us to win the World Cup," Pienaar stated afterwards when asked what the President told him. (Rekhy, 2019). The team famously went on to do just that.

There is no shortage of leadership and management advice out there. But leading is not just about following steps 1, 2, and 3 to become a good leader—it's about *leading with the heart* and tapping into the human side of leadership.

To be an effective leader, you need to lead with your heart and show the people you're leading that you care. It's about forming genuine, authentic connections with the people you lead rather than checking off a list of tasks or to-dos. Indeed, the wonderful Jeff Kaplan, an expert in leading with heart, states, "Leading with heart is NOT a goal-driven act but authentic. I come to the idea of being vulnerable."

From my experience as an executive coach and in conversations with experts in the area, I've found three ways leaders can lead with the heart. If you can make these mindset shifts as a leader, it will make an enormous difference in your teams and Organisations.

Lead don't manage. Employees don't need someone looking over their shoulders and micromanaging everything they do. Instead, they need someone who leads by example, shows integrity, and makes important guiding decisions for the Organisation. Employees need to have autonomy over their roles too. In research conducted by the University of Birmingham in the journal of work and occupations (Wheatly, 2017) researchers found a direct correlation between higher levels of autonomy in their work, well-being, and higher levels of job satisfaction."

Encourage, don't correct. Positive reinforcement and affirmation motivate people much more than correction or criticism. Focus on building people up by giving genuine compliments and encouraging them with what they're doing well. Gallup (Gallup, 2016) showed a recognition-rich environment is one of the best ways to make employees feel valued. The study says that recognition should not just be honest and authentic but also personalised to how each employee wants to be recognised.

Coach, don't tell. Instead of just telling people what to do and when to do it, come alongside them as a coach. Coaches empower people to make decisions, learn and grow, or go after opportunities. Be a champion of the people you lead by coaching and mentoring them.

Leading with heart is important and very lacking in the workplace right now. But if we want positive, effective, and efficient workplaces, we need to lead with our hearts! It brings back humanity and genuine, authentic connection to our workplaces which motivates people to do their best in their roles. Leading with heart is a mindset shift, but almost anyone can do it if they follow some clear principles.

LEADING WITH HEART AND THE WONDERFUL DR JEFF KAPLAN

As we have seen, the evolving paradigm is one that respects that business (work) and people (humanity) are interconnected and interdependent, as opposed to being viewed as separate entities coming together only to turn a profit.

I could not write about Leading with Heart without speaking to Dr Jeff Kaplan and Mark C Crowley. Dr Jeff is a Master Certified Coach and one of the leading experts in organisational coaching and coaching executives in the world, and Mark C Crowley is a world leader in leading with heart. They also happen to practise what they preach.

I asked Jeff what "Leading with Heart" truly means, and he told me that it was based on five major tenets:

Jeff: The first, as you might expect, is leading with empathy. Do you appreciate it, and can you put yourself in the feelings of others?
The second is leading with purpose. You will have heard the term servant leadership. Are you leading with a real

focus on the mission of the organisation and serving the clients out of its strategic intention?

The third is leading with humility. Is it about what's best for the organisation and not necessarily what's best for you?

The fourth: Are you engaged with not just the people but the work across all levels?

And the fifth is understanding. Do you understand the impact your decisions are having on the people and on the business?

Rachel: How important do you think a coaching leadership style is going to be as we see hierarchies collapsing and we're moving from command and control to collaborating and cultivating?

Jeff: One of the quickest ways to demotivate a group of employees is to do a performance review, and one of the best ways to develop and motivate employees is to teach them coaching skills. Performance reviews which can be painful-in part because people don't have the training or experience to do them right- are often like a logistical checking off-the-box kind of thing, while coaching conversations should be happening the entire year. Work is done with and through people, not despite them. You learn to have conversations with people so that you develop, motivate, inspire, and hold them accountable. Starting with the heart means, 'How are you doing? You are normally an amazingly productive person, and something has been happening in the last couple of weeks.' It means starting there rather than on the business.

Rachel: What would you say is the bottom line in terms of the changes we see in these times?

Jeff: Larger organisations are not going to thrive or even survive if they don't figure this piece out. More now than ever, we need people who lead with heart.

LEADING WITH HEART – MARK C CROWLEY – WHY WE NEED MORE LOVE AT WORK

Being a curious girl and having a big heart, I decided that I had to interview another great "Hearter". Mark C Crowley is another legend in this space. Mark wrote the incredible book Lead from the Heart – Transformational Leadership for the 21st Century (Crowley, 2022) I was grateful that Mark, like Jeff, was also willing to give time, space and energy to share his views.

Rachel: I'd love to explore if I may a little more about leading with heart. Could you articulate in your own words what is leading with heart?

Mark: That's a very big question, obviously. But you know I think the big premise is that we think we're rational beings. Descartes said, 'I think therefore I am'. And so, we think, 'Yes, that's me. I'm a human. I'm a thinker. I'm rational. I keep my emotions out there'.

My book's second edition came out in August 2022, but in the first edition, 11 years ago, I made the statement that we're not rational beings at all. And now there is a preponderance of data, new research that's coming out. In fact, two books came out that year and completely confirmed this.

What it means is that we're influenced heavily. Up to 95% of our time, our behaviour is influenced by something that we're feeling, not by something we're thinking. So, the thought comes in after the feeling in many cases. So, if that's the case, then if I say to you, 'Well, Rachel, if you do a good job, you know we're going to get better customer service scores,'—it goes to the head.

Then if you say, 'Well, you know our share price is going to get higher,'—it goes to the head. But if you say, 'You know, as part of you working for me, I'm going to help develop you, and I'm going to coach you, and I'm going to help you achieve what you set out to achieve at work'. That creates a feeling, 'Hello, I'm working for somebody that cares about me!'

And then the mind gets involved and says, 'Well, I want to do good work for this person because this person cares for me!' And that's how human beings operate. We reciprocate in that way; it has to be authentic. It can't be manipulated.

But basically, what I'm saying is that if we're wrong, if we're not rational beings, then we need to give people the emotional experiences that influence them to do the things that we're looking for. So, it has to be a win-win.

So, if I value you, if I respect you, if I make you feel safe, I appreciate you, if I'm growing and coaching you and giving you emotional and psychological safety and all those kinds of things, I'm setting you up for optimal performance. Because you, as a human being, are hard-wired to thrive on positive emotions, and I'm giving them to you in spades—you're just marinating in positive emotions!

And life is hard enough, so you're going to get your negative emotions just by people not getting you what you need or changing direction, or something happening that's negative in the world. You know, people say, "Oh well, you know you're over emphasising positive emotions."

I'm thinking, 'Who do you know that is so thriving in positive emotions that you know they're not struggling with life in some aspect?' It just doesn't happen.

So, I call that emotional currency, so rather than paying people in dollars, you know what we have to do. I'm saying that what really matters to people are emotional experiences.

And so, if you're doing the things that I just described translates into a currency, and people are being paid, if you will. They're being given these experiences. And it sets people up for optimal performance, and I proved it over and over and over.

Rachel: I love that term 'emotional currency'. What an incredible term. So that leads me to my next question: You and I both worked in the financial services industry for many years. What would the analysts do if we could show proof that leading with heart and giving more emotional currency could improve the share price of organisations?

Mark: Well, I think there's plenty of evidence that that's the case. I think there's some cynicism. If you went to Business School, you were taught how to manipulate a financial and, you know basically any financial tool on an income statement balance sheet; you were taught how to manipulate those, right?

So, if you have to hit your quarterly number, you're going to have to do something; you're going to have to sell something or buy something. And so, what happened is that we sort of depersonalise. We called people assets instead of human beings; we called them assets.

So, when you're looking at an asset, and you're looking at it— and by the way we treat them as a liability—they show up as a liability. So, if you're a CFO and you're thinking, 'Well, these people are costing me all this money,' instead of saying, 'No, these are the people that are driving the revenue', and people are a drag on earnings. So, when things weren't going well, companies just quickly said, 'Well, let's just let people go. Let's just lay them off!' Not understanding the emotional component of you just undermined, you know, my spirit.
But then it really undermines their ability to make a living and their trust in other people. Because I've been working really hard, and now just because the company is struggling, I have to go, 'Are you going to let me go?

Based on that? You're not going to keep me around and ask me to help you rebound?' And it's perverse. But we've done this for so long. It's led to the great resignation.

People just don't have trust in employers. And when employers say to me, 'You know, I just can't believe people!' And I'm like, 'Well, we should look back on your practices over the last 20-30 years and realise that whether it was you or you know somebody in your previous role, the role that you're in previously, but your organisation has made decisions like this'.

If I'm a millennial and I saw my mum and dad get fired during the Great Recession or let go during COVID, I'm not going to trust employers anymore. I'm not going to be looking for loyalty or real commitment. It's going to be transactional.

So, we've done real harm to people, and the interesting thing is that you can remedy this by starting to care about people truly caring about them, and they will.

To your point, we know plenty of evidence shows that organisations where people are authentically consistently cared about. Where the first decision isn't to let them go. If the company is struggling, it's to rally the troops and ask them to cut costs and figure out innovations to get us through these problems.

Those are the companies that will thrive, and those are the companies that get greater stock performance.

Rachel: So, we know that the hypothesis is true, and we can prove the hypothesis. But let's imagine you're an organisation, a large organisation, and suddenly you've come to the awareness—I need to do something as a leader. I need to bring in leading with heart into my organisation to make it more sustainably performant. What does that CEO do? What would be their first step, Mark?

Mark: It's not a light switch; it's a massive behavioural change. Because, you know, our traditional leadership theory says to pay people as little as possible and squeeze as much out of them as possible.

And to my way of thinking, neither one of those is an effective strategy because it undermines well-being. And the minute you undermine well-being, there's no way you're going to get people to perform at their best level because they're not feeling safe and they're always looking around—when's the next shoe to drop?

It's that kind of ambiguity, and so if a CEO comes out and says, 'You know, we're losing thousands of people every month. They're quitting this company, and we need to do something different, and you people, you need to be more empathetic, and you need to be more compassionate, and you need to be better coaches. And they're going to go, 'What? What are you talking about?'

And we're saying it's like you've been running a chicken restaurant for 30 years, and you're telling everybody, 'No more chicken, we're selling pizza'. And they're like, 'But I'm not good at pizza, I don't even know how to do that thing in the air, and I'm a chicken guy!' And so, you're saying I need you to be a pizza guy. I need you to be a pizza guy quickly, and you need to shift.

And it's threatening to people. So, the key is that it has to be a long-term commitment, and we have to teach managers that this is good. That this is going to get you better performance, and people aren't going to take advantage of you, and you're not going to look stupid and all the fantasies that people have about what I'm talking about.

And to understand that when you really care about people and you share your knowledge with them, and you create trusting environments that people will spawn in really positive ways, you have to. And this is controversial for some people, but not everybody is going to make the trip.

There's going to be people that are like, 'I'm chicken all the way. I've been successful by making chicken. And I have no reason to be a pizza guy. I'm a chicken guy, and I'm going to stick with that'.

And if you're in a pizza restaurant and all the guys doing is talking about chicken, and he's not doing anything to move in the direction of the pizza, well, he's not really aligned with what the company is trying to do.

So, you have to give that person an opportunity to learn the pizzas. To commit to getting good at it. Time to do that. Coaching to do that. And if they can't, you need to weed them out. Because of the toxicity that comes with people that are like, 'I don't even like pizza. I don't like caring about people—that's not my job. My job is to get performance in any way, shape, or form. So, if I have to manage with fear, I'm going to manage with fear. I don't need to coach people; they need to do it on their own. They're getting the bonus. They're lucky to have a job all that kind of thinking'.

This is what has pervaded in our business for a long time. So now you're going out, and you're like, I need you to be empathetic; now I need you to be compassionate. They're like, 'I don't even have those tools like either, right? It's not even in my being'. So, we need to say, 'Off you go. You know you can't manage people or human beings anymore unless you can make that transition'.

Rachel: So, in my next to last question—if there was a leader out there that says, 'I really want to change something about myself tomorrow, and I want to start the process of leading with heart,' what could they do?
What could they do that's easy and simple to start that process, recognising it is a journey, but what could they do tomorrow?

Mark: The easiest thing is apparently the hardest thing to do. So, it's thanking and appreciating people. We have this idea that if, Rachel, if I say to you, 'Hey, thank you for meeting the goal last month that I set for you. I really appreciate it. Oh, and thank you also for the report that you did a couple of weeks ago. That was very well done. I could see you really put a lot of time and energy into it. It really helped me... and oh, by the way, I came in the other day, and there was fresh coffee in the kitchen, and I know you brought that in, and I just want you to know how much I appreciate it'.

So now I thanked you three times for three different things. Somehow, we've got it in our mind that, now, in response, you're going to slack off like you're going to go, 'Oh, he thinks I'm doing a good job, so now I don't have to work anymore'. And it's stupid!

So, we hold back. It's like we're reaching into our pockets every time we're going to thank someone. It's like it's going to cost me somehow.
And what I've discovered is, is that you can never over-appreciate somebody. So, if I thank you for those three things, how would you feel? How would you feel if I thanked you for the report, for the meeting goals, and for bringing in coffee?

Rachel: Love it because it is recognition and that you know part of who we are as human beings, isn't it?

Mark: Do you feel compelled to cheat me now and to manipulate me or take advantage of me?

Rachel: On the contrary. You are building trust with me, and giving honest, direct critical feedback also can build trust...trust is about authentic feedback with good intent.

So, let's imagine that this goes viral, and you've got one message to send to the world, Mark. What's the one message that you would love to send to the world of leadership?

Mark: You know, it's a high hurdle for some people because they think it's soft or weak. Or like there's something wrong with him, but is it really?

It boils down to when I appreciate you for bringing the coffee and for getting your report done well and on time and meeting your goals; what I'm giving you is love. That's an experience of love. Those are the emotions that you feel when I say, 'You know, that was thoughtful of you to bring that coffee. And I love that kind of coffee, and I just was so happy when I came in, and you brought it. So, thank you'.

When you hear that from me, that feeling goes right to your heart, and it's love. All positive emotions translate into love.

So, if you understand that, you never have to go up and go, 'Hey, Rachel, I love you'. You just show it by being thoughtful enough to acknowledge the coffee in the report and the meeting the goals. Or saying, 'Hey, Rachel, I was reading this article over the weekend, and it's something you and I talked about, so I cut it out, and I have it for you. I think you'll love reading it'.

And it might not even be about, you know, financial services. It might be about gardening because you mentioned that you love to garden. How does that make you feel? It's like, 'Mark thinks about me like. I'm not just at work, he's at home on the weekend, and he's thinking about me when he's reading a gardening article'.

How does that make me feel? That's love. So, love your people is the answer to that question. That's really what it comes down to.

HEARTQ – HEART INTELLIGENCE AND HEARTMATH®

One of the core pin components of the HenkaQ model incorporates Heart Intelligence, or as I refer to it in this book: "HeartQ."

HeartQ *– Empathy and Connection- This is all about creating a climate of trust and connection through listening, asking vs telling, and getting furiously curious for and with others. It's about seeing things from multiple perspectives, fostering inclusion, and inviting others' participation. People feel seen and heard*

I propose that Heart Intelligence is going to be a lead factor in a growing need for what's become known as "global coherence." Global coherence seems to be the linchpin for adapting to rapid current world changes-- technological and otherwise—which calls for vast networks of global interconnectivity. I have come to think of HeartQ as a kind of global language that we would all benefit from learning.

There is an organisation based in the USA called the HeartMath® Institute. The HeartMath® Institute is a global research and educational organisation that uses a system called the HeartMath® system, which refers to various methods, tools, and techniques, based on a predominantly natural scientific foundation. Something called coherence is a key concept of the HeartMath® research.

HeartMath® research suggests that psycho-physiological coherence, which can be facilitated by positive emotions and or heart-focused breathing at about six breaths per minute, can, in turn, facilitate social coherence and ultimately vast global interconnectivity (McCraty, 2015) The punchline; if you can control your heart coherence, you can control how you show up. Leadership is all about how you show up.

HeartMath® tools and techniques really help you access the intelligence of the heart. And in fact, we hear from people across the world, spanning all professions, that attention to heart intelligence leads to better choices in the moment and confidence in navigating these stressful times.

Fundamentally, humans do not like change, especially unexpected change or change that we're not in control of. One of the challenges I often see in my executive coaching is that stress, anxiety, and overwhelm are out of hand, which is due to so many changes happening. The HeartMath® Institute says that one of the most effective ways to really reduce stress, anxiety, and even feelings of overwhelm is to learn how to access the heart's intelligence and shift the heart's rhythms, which sends a different neural message to the brain.

It is a scientific fact that the heart sends more information through the nervous system to the brain than the other way around, which might sound like a new discovery. This fact has been known since the late 1800s. The quality of the signals sent from the heart to the brain has profound effects on brain function, giving more mental clarity and reduced feelings of anxiety, stress, and overwhelm. HeartMath® tools and techniques are designed to get the rhythms of the heart more in synch. The effect: It changes the ascending information from the heart to the brain, which is necessary to establish a new baseline.

When we get our systems coherent and have the alignment between heart and brain, that's really when we access that deeper intuition that we have within our guidance, so we have a new sense of clarity and can easily make decisions which might otherwise appear complex.

COMMUNICATING WITH HEART – THE CONVERSATION

Effective organisations are networks of conversation, and the quality of those conversations is key. --Yvonne O'Reilly

Yvonne O'Reilly is a dear friend. She also happens to be a Master Coach and is an expert practitioner in transformational team coaching. Yvonne has a deep understanding of complex organisational systems and how to work with the invisible dynamics that help or hinder change.

Yvonne believes "Conversations must be a systemic endeavour and cannot simply be the exclusive domain of the CEO. A lot can be gained by having a coaching conversation with the CEO, but the CEO is the person who often knows least about the organisation, and they don't see what others see unless they are open to those conversations. The CEO is the tip of the pyramid and what they see is so little of what's going on at the base.

So, I asked Yvonne, "What is the magic of HeartQ?"

Yvonne: There is magic when we meet people as they are, with their absolute desire to connect with others, not just to connect ideas but to connect emotionally. People build connections through conversation. When we put a spotlight on the quality of relationships, magic does emerge. Looking at this from a systemic point of view, my sense check is that there's a conversation happening on the surface which be enriched through coaching skills.

But there is also a conversation under the surface, and that's the most important conversation. The magic lies in how we create a safe space so that people can bring their real emotions to the surface without feeling rejected, criticised, or judged. It is only then that real conversations can take place.

HEARTQ COMPETENCIES - HENKA LISTENING

A few years ago, a retired airline pilot approached me for coaching. He wanted to find new meaning in life in retirement by becoming a counsellor for young people and was struggling to connect with it emotionally.

Our first three sessions didn't go that well, but it was difficult for me to pinpoint exactly what the problem was. During our fourth session, however, everything changed. Previously, he seemed attentive, and he would give me ample opportunity for input, but I always felt that my input fell on deaf ears. As it turned out, that was exactly the problem.

He was obviously not physically deaf, but he didn't hear. He had retired as the captain of large commercial passenger planes--he was, in effect, God while on duty. From years at the helm, he was accustomed to taking charge and giving instructions; the lives of everybody on board were his responsibility.

The turning point in our coaching came with his realising that the new context of his environment called for a different kind of listening. He excelled at understanding the wholeness of his physical environment when he was a pilot—taking in data and reading fast-changing circumstances-- and now he had to apply that same level of understanding and develop a complete awareness of the wholeness of human communication. Remember the Situational Awareness lesson from the fighter pilot mentioned above? This retired pilot needed to learn human SA!

For many people, listening is just a verb involving our sense of hearing (our ears) and nothing more. Henka listening, however, denotes that the true art of listening lies beyond the verb's superficial meaning,

Do you really understand something completely when you listen with only your ears? Practically, you might say, "Yes, of course!". In my own experience as a coach, it takes so much more than just your ears to truly hear what someone is saying. In fact, when I trained as a coach, this was the movement that took me the longest to truly master. It is worth mentioning that brain coach Jim Kwik talks about silent and listen being anagrams of each other – naturally, one, being silent, is a prerequisite for the other.

Steve Hamilton-Clark talks passionately about listening when he talks about coaching 'I am convinced that listening is THE most critical coaching skill of all. As human beings, we need to be listened to.'

THE JAPANESE SYMBOL FOR LISTENING

I love the Japanese symbol for listening (Kiku). It is pure wisdom and a core part of the Henka philosophy. It involves not only the ears (to hear) but also the mind (to think), the heart (to feel), the eyes (to see) and undivided attention to focus.

The Ears to Hear

The ability to hear is a matter of simple human biology. Scientifically speaking, we hear through our auditory

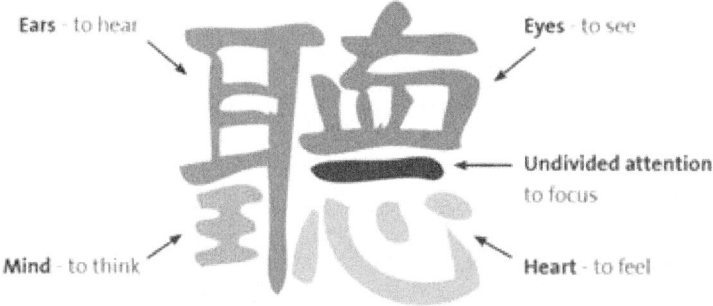

nerves. Japanese symbol consists of two parts one an ear and outside the lines and entrance gate. Together our ears are the entrance gate with sound or words.

On the other hand, our capability to listen differs from our shallow understanding of hearing. Listening is a skill that needs to be nurtured and cannot be attained by simply hearing something.

Although hearing allows us to listen, the process of listening is so much more than hearing.

The Mind to think

Our minds allow us to listen beyond just decoding sound combinations. Our minds interpret everything that we have heard, felt, seen, and all-in-all listened to in the past in relation to what is heard now at the moment. Sometimes, our minds even can interpret something that was unspoken.

"A good head and a good heart are always a formidable combination." – Nelson Mandela

The Heart to Feel

Our hearts allow us to feel. This is the very crucial part of listening. According to Gregg Braden: *"The heart is where the action is."*

The Eyes to See

Just like the ear's capacity to hear, the eye takes in images so that we can physically see. But seeing things holistically requires deliberate practice. Sometimes, we don't even need our eyes to really see.

My friend Carole has a visual disability. Most people would be completely unaware that she had this condition. And yet Carole can see what others can't see. Her listening is deeper than anyone I know. She can "see" clearly, penetratingly. Carole happens to be French, and curiously the translation of "clear indication" in French is clairvoyance.

In other words, getting beyond the outer aspects of a thing or a person and instead reaching towards its/their inner aspects will give you a truer "picture of what/who you're actually looking at. This, of course, is the holistic view that we believe helps one see more clearly.

Undivided Attention to Focus

We live in a world of tremendous noise, so becoming distracted is becoming ever easier.

It's another form of breakdown that is occurring in our post-modern world and granted, it is hard to overcome the trend towards fractured attention, especially when trying to cope with a host of other troubles. Still, cultivating the art of undivided attention keeps us on track and can help us live more effectively.

To listen in this way, you absolutely need to free yourself from any kind of distractions. This skill is not one that can be attained overnight. It is a skill that needs to be constantly honed.

Practice does make [more] perfect. Listening well is not something you "get" once and master on the spot in the same way that going to the gym once or twice will not make you fit or your muscles built. A BIG NO! As with the gym, so is quality listening: Use it, or you lose it. And this is why it is often the most difficult of coaching skills to acquire—because it requires patience and persistence. When you have mastered each part of the Japanese symbol for listening—absorbing with all your faculties what is being communicated -- you will now be able to "see clearly." This is where the word clairvoyance comes from. So, apply every component of active listening, and you may very well be on your way to what I call corporate clairvoyancy!

Corporate Clairvoyancy is very important in this murky and volatile world. It allows us to see more clearly as we struggle to detect the way through struggles. Developing this capacity can keep us on track. Attaining a clear way of looking at things helps us to solve problems effectively, whether it's a business problem, a societal problem, or even a global problem.

INCLUSION

My last point on HeartQ relates to one of the most important outcomes – inclusion. To be sustainably performant, organisations need diverse thoughts from the board and throughout the organisation. LGBTQ+ Leader Pips Bunce had been through the Henka training programme and wrote a blog with her colleagues Jesper Dissing and Lisa Dickson. She said: "Coaching as a tool is a powerful method to allow people's inclusive leadership abilities to foster and flourish" (Pips Bunce, 2022).

Coaching will allow you to explore your leadership response and help you define how you will disrupt the status quo. It will allow you to help create the right conditions where everyone can thrive, irrespective of their point of difference, their dimensions of diversity or any other aspect that means they may be disadvantaged through non-inclusive leadership.

To bring inclusive leadership to life, there are many coaching skills that can be used to galvanize the importance of inclusive leadership. Be this through using powerful questions to explore these themes, understanding the coachees' values, assigning metaphors, exploring perspectives, and bringing to life the biases that may exist that are inhibiting the coachee from truly empowering those around them. The transformation will be incredible."

HeartQ is a critical part of the Henka Paradigm. The heart, as we discovered earlier if we look at the science, is a brain.

The next chapter discusses another key brain, our gut or as we call it hunger!

CHAPTER 5

HungerQ –Purpose, Passion and Belief

'... [A] research study on managers conducted by Google revealed that the number one most important behaviour of the highest-scoring managers was that they're effective coaches. This meant that they listened, guided, and helped their people grow' (from The Buddha and the Badass: The Secret Spiritual Art of Succeeding at Work by Vishen Lakhiani). (Lakhiani, 2020)

Mac Anderson famously said, "Belief fuels Passion and passion rarely fails".

Another word for passion could be desire.

In his famous book, Think and Grow Rich, Napoleon Hill defines desire as **'the starting point of all achievement, not a hope, not a wish, but a keen pulsating desire, which transcends everything.'**

At Henka, we use the term HungerQ.

HUNGERQ – THE INTELLIGENCE OF PURPOSE, PASSION, AND BELIEF

HungerQ – Purpose, Passion, and Belief – This part of the Henka model is about harnessing these vital qualities. It begins with healthy emotional self-regulation, having a clear sense of purpose, believing in oneself, believing in others, being acutely aware of one's and others' strengths, persistently being acutely aware of one's and others' strengths, persistently keeping the big picture in mind, and mindfully managing your energy, not your time.

So how does this fit with coaching?

When I started to train to become a coach, I was somewhat clueless about what coaching really was. Tony Robbins was the only coach I had heard of, and he swore quite a bit (which I liked).

Firstly, I confused coaching with mentoring; secondly, I had presumed that coaching was all about *action*; finally, I thought you had to be able to give lots of profound advice.

I was completely wrong on all counts.

I very quickly realised on the road to becoming a Coach that the first lesson learnt was that it was not about me as Coach but the Coachee. Coaching enables a Coachee to think for him or herself, explore alternatives, question his/her actions, and discover new alternatives.

It started to make sense to me that Coaching was like an irrigation system. You could go to the end of the tap and use a hose to water a single bed in your garden…better still, take the same hosepipe, add a couple of little sprinklers, open it, and you can water the whole garden at the same time. It is unleashing the full potential of a human being.

COMMAND AND CONTROL
OR PURPOSE AND SERVICE

While this discussion is incomplete without including the human spirit and spiritual intelligence (addressed in the following chapter), let's at least consider two diverging perspectives regarding what "company growth" means. Some people might say that humanity has advanced and prospered greatly under shareholder capitalism and an unlimited growth paradigm that equates purpose with profit or maximising shareholder value (Friedman, A

Theoretical Framework for Monetary Analysis, 1970) Others would say it has resulted in negative economic, environmental, and social side effects including income disparity, financial crises, accounting frauds, the depletion of global resources, and climate change (Hurth, 2018) (Peele, 2019) (Williams, 2019)

Traditionally, leaders have been motivated by their own self-interest to increase their own influence, profit, and position. Additionally, according to Peter Block in his book Stewardship, many companies still have "healthy residues" of direct command-and-control systems in their contemporary attitudes about money (Block, 2013).

In the new leadership paradigm, purpose, passion, and belief (HungerQ) take front and centre stage. In the new leadership paradigm, leaders are driven to make long-lasting, intrinsically valuable improvements to people's lives and societies. In other words, they prioritise serving the organisation or community before their own immediate interests. Profit thus becomes less important than meaning or purpose. It is not just millennial workers that place a high value on this. Baby boomers and Gen Xers are not immune from being purpose-driven, as studies have demonstrated.

At its core, this new leadership paradigm is guided by ideas like transparency, compassion, and service. Although some may view these ideas as "soft methods," there is proof that outcomes are driven by progressive leadership beliefs. In fact, managerial openness is the top factor influencing employee satisfaction, according to one poll on employee engagement. Teamwork and cooperation, ideas anchored in purpose-driven leadership, were rated as the top qualities that employees admire most in their co-workers in the same poll. According to another report, employee trust significantly influences engagement, workplace satisfaction, job quality, and employee retention.

We need to re-evaluate our long-held assumptions about why a corporation exists, especially considering the growth of customers concerned with the common good. "You want a tale that motivates workers, thrills partners and draws in clients.

A Henka leader works on connecting the coachee with a purpose.

A famous story highlights this. President John F. Kennedy made his first trip to NASA in 1962. While taking a tour of the building, he came across a janitor walking down the corridor with a broom in hand. When the President casually inquired what he did for NASA, the janitor answered, "I'm helping put a man on the moon.".

INDIVIDUAL BELIEFS AND BRUCE LIPTON

I could not talk about belief without first acknowledging the work of Bruce Lipton, who, in 2006, wrote the influential book, *The Biology of Belief.*

The book is a courageous deep dive into the biochemical effects of brain functioning. Bruce demonstrates how all cells in the body are affected by thoughts.

His suggestion, with which I concur, is that most of our beliefs are programmed within the first seven years of our lives. That is when our brains are operating in what is called Theta mode. To get an idea of where Lipton's philosophy goes, let's see, right out of the gate, what working with biology of belief looks like. He suggests that there are four ways in which we might be able to reprogram beliefs:

Repetition. By feeling and experiencing rituals of all habits, we can achieve the act of reprogramming.

Hypnosis. A coach can facilitate a process in which the mind is brought into a low vibrational frequency as well as assist with changing beliefs.

High Impact Event Programming can be rewritten after a traumatising life experience, cf. James and his heart attack or Covid.

Energy Psychology Belief Modification Programs (or "Super Learning") can engage the brain's super learning processes.

I have seen all four of these influences play out in my own personal life experience. But what impact might reprogramming beliefs have on organisations?

ORGANISATIONAL BELIEFS

Operational guides, procedure manuals, and protocols are found in most organisations.

Every organisation is also guided by a certain set of beliefs. Compared to any written manual, these beliefs have a much, much greater impact on the effectiveness of the system. Sometimes, however, these convictions may eventually result in an uncontested status quo. They stop being optional ways of thinking and become unquestionable facts.

The shared beliefs and assumptions that have developed over a long period of time comprise the subconscious of an organisation. If an organisation is accomplishing objectives, people are enjoying their jobs, and performance is sustainable. This is wonderful.

What if, however, the subconscious nature of a particular organisation is derailing corporate transformation programmes?

This is where the Henka model comes in, and the Henka Method for Cultural Transformation™ is discussed and explained in the next chapter.

Transforming an organisational culture requires change at the organisational belief level, which is much more complex than simply changing a few business processes.

As Bruce Lipton says, "Our beliefs control our bodies, our minds, and thus our lives…"

LISTENING TO YOUR GUT -

I think it is fair to say that today data rules the world in which we live.

We base our most important life decisions on facts, statistics, and algorithms, from hiring to investing to selecting a business partner. Knowing the value of quantitative evidence, it could seem unwise to rely on your instincts when making judgments.

That's wrong.

It's wrong because our gut has intelligence. Our stomach is packed with nerves and functions. It is an information processing system, and just like the heart, it is also a brain. The surfaces of the gut lining house around 100 million nerves that make up the enteric nervous system (ENS) which has a significant processing capacity.

Once upon a time, we relied heavily on intuition. For most of known time, it was a necessary function of survival. It may be argued that as dependency on machines, computers, data, and algorithms has increased, we see a decline in the use of the delicate but powerful faculty. In some instances, it appears to have atrophied altogether. But if it is a human being making decisions, intuition will vie to be heard because, unless you're Mr Spock on the Starship Enterprise, pure data will not get you to the promised land. We need the very human qualities of emotion and intuition; we need Captain Kirk. That is why Henka includes this form of intelligence in the discussion about aligning with passion, belief and purpose.

An article by Stephanie Vozza (Vozza, 2020) highlights the indispensability of instinct. Antonia Hock, global head of *The Ritz-Carlton Leadership Center*, says, "Instinct is a powerful data point that can be a treasure trove of untapped generational knowledge in decision making." And we hear further from Holland-Kornegay, who says, "A gut feeling is the result of a huge number of cognitive processes occurring in your brain, sizing up new sensory information against past experiences and coming to a prediction."

Brené Brown (Brown, 2010) also states in her book, *The Gifts of Imperfection,* that one of your best tools for making decisions is intuition. Unfortunately, a lot of individuals have trouble believing in their instincts.

Brené says that it is partly since most people don't know what intuition is. They perceive it as an instinctual sensation unrelated to logic or reason. In truth, reason and intuition may work together.

"But why would you want to believe your gut feeling? Simply put, by doing so, you can get over your fear of taking risks. Risk-taking and its boon to creativity is often a game-changer in terms of both individual and company growth. Can you begin to see how bringing our intuition on board can transform the subconscious nature of an organisation and enhance transformation programmes?

Most individuals want to avoid danger and uncertainty, which causes them to hesitate and make bad choices. Learning to trust your intuition can help you become used to acting in the face of ambiguity and overcome the anxiety of choosing the wrong course of action.

Put simply, beliefs shape individuals and determine how they rock, how they roll, how they succeed, and how happy they are. We all have beliefs, and most of these are held in our subconscious. It is when our beliefs inform our intuition that impacts our effectiveness in leading.

Whilst we are warned about our own tendencies for "fallacious thinking" and "biases," it turns out that one's gut feeling can be the most important 'data' of all.

Yet, the fact remains listening to our gut has undergone a fall from grace. The (holistic) Henka approach ensures that intuition is reinstated to its rightful place in decision-making and leading.

A PRACTICAL GUIDE FOR ENLISTING INTUITION

The Henka Leader as Coach teaches the importance of listening and trusting your gut. The voice in your gut is wise, and it can push you to do something that feels right when another option might have paid better results. The truth is you need to be listening to the gut, the head, the heart and the spirit (coming up next) to calculate the best leadership move.

Aileen MacLaren, a senior HR leader and one of the early Henkees, brilliantly dubbed this "muddyleadership" (drawing upon a rugby theme, as in getting down in the dirt and roughing it with the team-- no ivory towers here) which has now become part of Henka folklore

In conducting business, the question is, is it better to stick with the hard facts, or should intuition play a major role in decision-making? It's complicated, especially when factors ranging from emotional to external pressures could sway our intuition at any given time. We may be tempted to rely on intuition to arrive quickly at a conclusion when overwhelmed and then end up overlooking important steps that may come back to haunt us later.

Another point to be aware of when it comes to listening to your gut is how to distinguish its healthy, productive form from the misleading unconscious bias. This, for example, can sway a decision in hiring that can carry long-term ramifications.

Of course, for any major deal or business transaction, your instincts should be supported by facts and figures and be considered only after thoroughly analysing the relevant data.

The most reliable formula seems to be when logic and reason are applied first, with intuition and instinct coming in to round out the overall assessment.

One of my clients conducted an interview for a prospective employee who had great credentials on his application. A certain uneasy sense allowed her to take time to consider some other points that came up in the interview. Her intuition led her to dig deeper. She made a few follow-up calls and, based on new facts that she learned, realized the person was not a good fit for the company. The synergistic effect of merging data review with healthy instinct gives leadership that extra edge.

Perhaps you heard some data about a new system or service that promises to give you a competitive edge. Now you have a choice: you can go ahead with a feeling about it (impelled perhaps by an urgency to succeed because of some unconscious bias), or you can gather more information and then invite your intuition in to make the final call.

EQ - EMOTIONAL INTELLIGENCE

Another essential factor in the purpose, passion and belief equation is Emotional Intelligence.

The capacity to recognise and control one's own emotions as well as those of others is referred to as Emotional Intelligence. It was first brought into mainstream consciousness by Daniel Goleman in his 1995 book ***Emotional Intelligence: Why It Can Matter More Than IQ*** (Goleman, Emotional Intelligence - Why It Can Matter More Than IQ, 1995) . Emotional awareness, or the capacity to recognise and name one's own emotions, the capacity to harness those emotions and apply them to activities like thinking and problem-solving, and the capacity to manage emotions, which entails both controlling one's own emotions when necessary and supporting others to do the same, are the skills that are typically considered to make up emotional intelligence.

Goleman breaks down EQ into five components:

1. Self-awareness
2. Self-regulation
3. Motivation (closely related to passion, perhaps even synonymous)
4. Empathy
5. Social skills

I decided to look at 1 and 2 in more detail

THE POWER OF AWARENESS

You will have perhaps noted this word throughout the book. Awareness. Awareness might well be considered the overall factor in aligning with purpose, passion and belief. The reality is that none of us can possibly begin to transform or act unless we are aware of our behaviour, what might be holding us back, what our emotions are, and what is going on in our physiology. Equally, no organisation can transform unless it is entirely aware of what the real challenge is.

Dr Mike Watson stated: "you don't simply create meaning; you yourself are meaning. And, because you and the world are ever-changing, what you mean to yourself, and others constantly changes. Therefore, the more self-aware you are, the more you stay in alignment with purpose."

What is critical for any individual working in an organisation is that their own values and beliefs are aligned with those of the organisation. Failure to do that creates a toxic environment for the individual. The organisation survives, but the individual creates their own toxicity. The only alternative is for them to adapt or leave the system. So many people leave their positions naming "a toxic work environment" as the reason. As a leader, keeping your finger on the pulse of general levels of awareness, starting with self-awareness, can make all the difference.

PQ - POSITIVE INTELLIGENCE AND EMOTIONAL SELF REGULATION

The final intelligence under this category might seem like a no-brainer, but its impact cannot be underestimated, and that is Positive Intelligence or PQ. It acts as oil does for wheels making everything move along smoothly and pleasantly. The good news is that if you haven't been naturally endowed with this wonderful quality, it can be developed. This is true on an individual level as well as a corporate or organisational level. The ways in which a positive outlook relates to purpose, passion and belief are too many to name, but we could zero in on the research:

Shirzad Chamine wrote the wonderful book *Positive Intelligence* (Chamine, 2012) which expounds on why only 20% of teams and individuals reach their true potential. He talks about PQ, which is the Positive Intelligent Quotient. In simple terms, if somebody has a high PQ, this means that they have a higher ratio of positive outlook rather than a negative outlook. His book analyses many studies on happiness and the workplace and concludes that "higher PQ leads to higher salary and greater success in the areas of work, marriage, health, sociability, friendship, and creativity."

Chamine points out that your mind is your best friend and worst enemy. Positive intelligence is the relative strength of these two modes of your mind. As a result, positive intelligence is a measure of your mental control and how well your mind behaves in your best interests.

What really interests me is how we can develop high-performing cultures in organisations. This is not about casual Fridays, free cupcakes, or a pool table; this is about organisations providing opportunities for growth and ensuring support in the workplace. If you want to be a leader and leader as coach, then this is about supporting people to develop that control of their minds increasing their PQ.

Chamine suggests CEOs who have a higher PQ are much more likely to lead teams who report that the work climate sports high performance. Employees that have a high PQ take fewer sick days and are much less likely to burn out. Leaders with higher PQ are more accurate and careful in decision-making and need much less effort to get their work done.

PURPOSE, PASSION, AND BELIEF AS THE FOUNDATION OF CHANGE

Every structure needs a solid foundation, whether it's a small house or a towering skyscraper. Just as buildings are structures, so are organisations—and they, too, require a solid foundation to ensure that the structure can stand on its own.

Organisations should be built on a set of core values, principles, and a driving sense of purpose.

Let's say organisations have their core values laid down, crystal clear, for everyone to understand. These values might even be expressed in the form of vision and mission statements. But how real are they? Are the core values tangible, and are they really understood and lived? And here's the important part: core values are embodied in real people. In other words, people are your true foundation.

As hard as it is for some organisations to understand, people are not expendable. I believe that the HumanSpiritQ (coming up) part of the integrative HENKA model brings this unequivocally into every equation. They are priceless and a great asset if you treat them right.

The people at the top of an organisation generally name their core values by way of adjectives. For example, a school might say that their institution is built on "integrity, responsibility, excellence, and discipline" -- I-RED for short. Sure, it's catchy, but don't expect parroted words to mean much unless they manifest through the people at work.

Lindsey Braik, who heads global talent for The Henka Institute, once told me that in the 1980s, she was asked if she could recite the ten company values. She replied:

"Wouldn't it be better to be able to live them than to recite them?"

How true.

The Henka methodology helps organisations practise the type of leadership that individuals need. And this is what allows a person's sense of passion to be unleashed toward a mission whose core values they identify with. That's a very different animal than the person rattling off mission statements. Organisations cannot survive without people, and if you're looking for engagement and retention, then you must take care of their physical, emotional, and mental well-being. If that's the foundation, and the first floor is purpose, passion, and belief, then all that is built upon it is sturdy and full of potential. This is where coaching comes in, as these elements are often nurtured best through reflective guidance and encouragement.

Digging Deeper: The Foundation of the Individual

You might have noticed; we're journeying one level at a time towards the grassroots to identify what we need to do to transform organisations. We agree that organisations are built on people, but what is the foundation of the individuals who make up an organisation? In the foundation of a structured analogy, this is what a building inspector is concerned with.

People vary in character, personality, temperament, and style, which means that employees or team members are certain to be a varied bunch as well. Some are timid. Some are strong. Some are studious, while others are lazy. Just look again at Bill and Michael in Chapter 2. You see what I mean-- everyone is different!

And everybody responds to change differently. The constant, however, is **self-trust**. This is the most elemental building block we are looking for.

According to Erik Erikson, a German American developmental psychologist, the foundation of human development is trust in self and others.

Take note of the word "development." Development goes hand-in-hand with *change*. The question is how to move gracefully through change when, typically, people are resistant to change. The ones who overcome this propensity are those who trust in themselves and in others to develop into the best they can be. This component is crucial in the fast-changing environment we all face.

As the world rapidly transforms around us, we might contemplate why suicide rates are so high. Why do people seem to leave their workplaces much in the way a child flees from school? Why are we alone? Why are we depressed? It largely depends on self-trust, which, when compromised, chips away at your self-esteem and sense of identity. You lose your foundation. You lose you.

In contrast, the more self-possessed, at-ease-in-the-world types (likely nurtured by early security-inducing experiences) are freed up to explore what the world has to offer. Such a person approaches the world, others, and even other perspectives with more openness.

So, how do we prevent our foundation our self-trust-- from crumbling? From where can we bring in reinforcement—especially if self-trust is the elemental feature of or predictor for the ability to forge ahead, innovate, cooperate, and create—even as plates shift beneath?

COACHING FOR MASTERING CHANGE

We know that "change is the only constant in life" (as pointed out by the Greek philosopher Heraclitus). And as we pointed out above, people are normally resistant to change (as we know from observing everyone, including ourselves). If people are resistant to change, then it stands to reason that organisations, which are comprised of people, are resistant to change too. So how can we transform an organisation with this inherent handicap?

Coaching has the ability to reach down to the level of foundation and establish trust. And resistance falls away when trust of self and others flourishes. This reinforcement project begins with one individual and continues one individual at a time. The individual is the most fundamental building block – the grassroots of an organisation. We support the individual by supporting *their* foundation.

According to Calum Byers, an executive coach and team facilitator from the United Kingdom, if we change the process of how an individual thinks of him or herself in a rapidly changing world, we transform that person. While Byers' quote specifically refers to an organisation, it applies equally to the transformation of the individual. Additionally, Byers comments, "An organisation only transforms if the people actively open themselves to change." How does this happen? Really, the only way is through focused, intimate coaching of individuals in any organisation.

Coaching can help individuals open themselves to change. Coaching can boost their trust in themselves and their self-esteem, eventually leading to an enhanced approach towards others. This, of course, creates a different work environment.

According to Byers, coaches must understand the individual, treat them with positive regard, and believe in (trust) their ability to change. These are the elements through which the magic of coaching happens. This is where individuals become more open to productive, life-changing conversations. These are the conversations which aim to truly understand what motivates them.

This is how coaching paves the way for self-development and supports transformation.

Passion is key – or not

James was a customer service representative for a polling company in Australia. He told me that this job was not his passion at all. He was earning more than enough and said that this was the main reason why he got into this industry. James's passion was broadcasting, and he deeply regretted that money had so influenced his decision to pursue his current job.

During his first month, he performed admirably, but going into his second month; he performed horribly. His fifth month, somehow, showed an even worse performance. He was absent all the time, and his metrics were mostly in the red. His team leader knew something had to be done. In a call centre environment such as this, team leaders also act as the personal "coaches" of their respective team members. The team leader's name was Grace.

Grace was getting worried for James. She'd been coaching James every week for a few months now, and it seemed that there was no improvement in his performance. Something had to be done, or else James would be fired after six months because he was already on probation. As James told us, Grace did care about him and his future.

We began by explaining the Henka principles to Grace. Grace's coaching was more about "how-to" regarding the work, not on the person himself. She was coaching but was approaching it the wrong way. With Henka behind her, it seemed to James as if Grace had novel ideas about what came next. She was getting more "individual-centric," as James described it. She made sure to let him know that she believed in him and had believed in him since the first month of his employment. Grace put energy into developing more of a personal connection with James, and they became good friends. That was the beginning of when James started showing signs of improvement in his work. His average handling time went down, his attendance became almost perfect, and his metrics went up. In his seventh month, he got a promotion.

Let's follow the Henka trail through this episode to get a sense of the guideposts that bring a leader as coach, such as Grace, confidently through the process with James: HenkaQ easily accesses the Head (Mind), Heart, Hunger (gut/intuition) and Human Spirit (Soul). in a way that allows them to operate as Leader as Coach

- Henka's Q's—the holistic and integrative view of the person, allows Grace to move out of the myopic focus on 'how-to' regarding the work and onto the person himself. From this state, Grace accesses her broadest energy to lead. The (Head/Mind) is empowered from this standpoint.
- Grace's 'novel ideas' begin to come from her fluid movement through all quadrants. It's this leave-no-Q-behind attitude that gives rise to the next indication of where to move towards.
- Grace puts energy into communicating and developing more of a personal connection with James, which builds up HeartQ. She reminds herself that growth and change only happen when there's a relationship. (Heart).

- Providing a sense of belief in James boosted his SQ—the energy that comes from tapping into his individual (Spirit).
- Grace addresses the (Hunger) factor and helps James unleash his passion which is to pursue broadcasting. She also helps him manage the temporary chaos that this is likely to invite until he transitions into a new state of order— one that is more aligned with who he is and what he wants in life.

What's the takeaway from this episode? James became a very productive person just because he felt that somebody trusted him. His self-trust increased, and as that improved, so did his trust in his team, especially in his team leader. Once her coaching approach was right, it created a solid foundation of self-trust and enabled his transformation.

Hopefully, this gives a good sense of what the foundation (core values, the individual and trust) looks like. We also have a view of the various forms of intelligence and have explored ways of integrating the parts with the whole. Now we come to plug the whole thing into the outlet, so to speak.

This is where the body meets the soul.

In an organisation that appears to have a healthy spirit or soul, there you will find real respect for spiritual intelligence (SQ)—the crown of all intelligence. When a force higher than the CEO is acknowledged, respected, and drawn upon, and the human spirit is nurtured in an organisation, what you have is a truly vivified entity.

While the human spirit and spiritual intelligence have been referenced (at least as it relates to belief and passion), let's now take a deep dive into these terms. In a world where assets, acquisitions, regulations, and revenue are all terms used for progress and success, in the Henka world, values, courage, compassion, and wisdom are all markers as well for navigating towards the desired outcome. Working with spiritual intelligence can lead a corporation further, and deeper (more impact) than anyone involved could have imagined. They will prove indispensable for moving forward in our turbulent, complex, unpredictable world-- a compass for that new future on the horizon.

CHAPTER 6

HumanSpiritQ – Culture and Identity

The Henka Model™ - How to Achieve Sustainable Performance

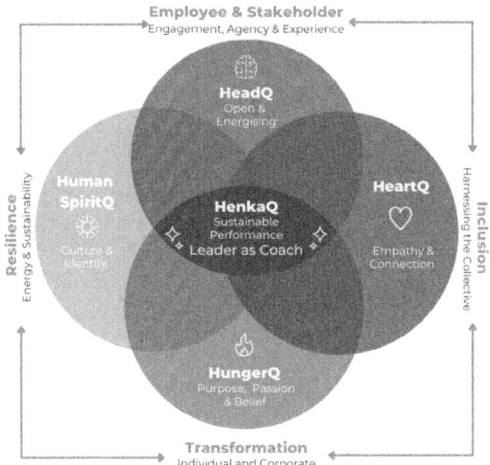

I was on holiday in southern Thailand. It has everything to make one feel safe and wonderful: beaches longer than you could ever imagine, massages in every direction, swimming pools, and the most amazing staff looking after my family and me. This was my third year at the same hotel with my ten-year-old.

One day I caught sight of another woman and... oh no...she was wearing the same bathing suit!

Every afternoon we were treated to the "5 o'clock club": the objective was to have as much food and drink during the two hours that the club was on. It was often raucous.

One evening I spotted a woman wearing the same bathing suit as me, and we chatted. It turned out her name was Angie, and she came from somewhere near Bristol and had been raised in Singapore. She was a hypnotherapist, so I asked her if hypnotherapy could help with weight loss. I was a hefty size 16, and I'd tried every diet under the sun, including Slimming World, Weight Watchers, various shakes, and French protein diets--you name it. Nothing had ever worked. She passed me her card, which read: *Holland Hypnotherapy* and said, "Holding onto weight was a way of protecting yourself".

I held onto the card for nine months.

THE POWER OF SOLUTIONS-FOCUSED HYPNOSIS

Something made me decide to ring her one day, and I embarked on my hypnosis journey. It turned out Angie was a clinical solution-focused hypnotherapist, which is based on the philosophy of solution-focused brief therapy, and, as her title suggests, she is concerned with addressing the solution rather than the problem. This technique is apparently very effective in the treatment of anxiety disorders, phobias, and depression, as well as weight loss.

In each session, I was asked the "Miracle Question", which encouraged me to contemplate and articulate how my present situation could be different. Insoo Kim Berg (1998), co-founder of Solution Focused Brief Therapy (SFBT), and her team experimented with the Miracle Question after listening to a client struggling to respond to straightforward questioning. The Miracle Question enables clients to imagine what would be different for them on waking if a miracle had come about that solved their problem while they had been sleeping.

Besides the Miracle Question, this hypnotherapy also used scaling. This rating system of 1-10 not only helped me track my progress but also accomplished three things:

1. It toned down my weight issue by limiting it within a manageable range. I stopped awfulizing about it being an off-the-charts issue.
2. Using scaling allowed me some emotional distance from the issue so that I wasn't so entangled in it. This got me to observe myself more objectively and with more thinking power.
3. Scaling broke up what seemed like a monster problem into manageable steps.

This system provided Angie and me with a frame of reference to work with to establish movement forward or backwards and map progress as the therapy continued.

The punchline is that I lost around nine kilos and have kept it off for three years! I now eat butter and cheese - and just don't worry about what I eat.

I was astounded at the transformation and thought to myself if this is *that* simple for an individual, then how simple could it be for groups, teams, and organisations? From this personal experience of transformation, the Henka™ Method for Group Transformation was born.

THE HENKA METHOD FOR CULTURAL TRANSFORMATION

I managed to win a large contract for an organisation that had made 22 acquisitions in 3 years. They were looking for support in sustainable transformation and engagement. I was confident the methodology would work (as it had for me in hypnotherapy) but was not entirely sure.

The organisation was global and so virtual facilitation was needed. The results were beyond anything I could have imagined

Using the method

There are a lot of methods of working with groups and doing group coaching. The Henka method is beautifully simple and can be used to give some structure to working on a particular topic.

As with individual coaching, you are focussing on exploring the people; it is their job to explore the topic. Here are the key elements:

- Look to create dialogue - exchange of meaning - in the group.
- Check for a common understanding of key ideas that are shared and concepts exploited, e.g., being 'tough' with low performance - what does that mean?
- Get commitment to the process upfront, return to that commitment and check if needed.
- If the session is going off-topic or seems to not be serving its aims, check back in with the group, and refer to the agreed structure.
- Regularly check the energy of the group.
- Help the group to be clear on what actions are owned by who at the end.

Create a Safe Space - design the alliance for the session, for the individual, group, or team. This could be done by a trust-building exercise that allows the group to experience what it is to co-create a way forward.

1) **Define the clear topic of discussion** - The facilitator defines an emotionally neutral topic for the group.
2) **What's great about the named topic that the company should do more of?** – Positive psychology plays an important role here and keeps the momentum going. (Powerful Questions, Listening, Curiosity, Challenge, Playback, Suspending Judgement, Being Present)
3) **Rating the topic on a scale from 1-10** – everyone gets the feeling of being heard. (The rating can be done anonymously.)
4) **Averaging the Score**
5) **Incremental Changes to improve** (What does it take to move from a 7 to 7.5, for example?) These are changes that you can influence--so-called quick fixes. (Powerful Questions, Listening, Curiosity, Challenge, Playback, Suspending Judgement - Be Present)
6) **Creativity – Challenge and Stretch** Introduce the question: What does it take to move from a 7 to a nine instead of a 7.5? - Implement skills as above but with an emphasis on Challenge and Stretch.

This requires blue-sky thinking; anything is possible!

7) **Commitment and Accountability**

Using this 8-step process helps build openness in a group across different hierarchical levels and functions. Everyone feels heard, and the momentum that is created speeds up the change process and allows for sustainable transformation.

HUMANSPIRITQ - SPIRITUAL INTELLIGENCE

Spiritual Intelligence is probably the part of the HenkaQ model that is the most challenging part for a leader to adopt, and I think the reason is due to corporate conditioning. As Hedda Pahlson-Moller, a global impact catalyst, articulated in her *Flex and the City* podcast, "Someone can be extremely kind at home but feels they have to turn into another animal once they arrive at work."

HumanSpiritQ – Culture and Identity - This is all about having a deep respect for the human spirit, making values-driven decisions, having the courage and resilience to balance getting things done and developing people, and demonstrating compassion and wisdom.

The term Spiritual Intelligence (SQ) has gained momentum in the last few years, with many incredible researchers and authors writing books on the subject.

In researching this topic, I came across the kind and magnanimous Dr Mike Watson who had conducted his Doctorate thesis on Spiritual Intelligence. I wanted to explore Spiritual Intelligence in a language that might resonate with the largest audience. To that end, I framed my questions to Mike to consider the perspective of someone like my own mum, who is not religious and a very straightforward North Englander.

One of the things I was looking to address is that people are reluctant to utter the word "spirituality" or invoke "spiritual intelligence" in a workplace (as if it was unprofessional).

Rachel: Mike, if you were explaining to my mum the meaning of spiritual intelligence, what would you say to her?

Mike: I would say spiritual intelligence is the culmination of all our intelligence that we can utilise to be wise and compassionate in any situation.

Rachel: That's beautiful. If someone is an atheist, could they have SQ?'

Mike: There is no need to mix the concept of spirituality with a belief system [with all the cultural trappings] because from the perspective of spiritual intelligence, we are only acknowledging that there is a force and a purpose that we have that is greater than ourselves.
[Think the universality of the 12-step programs].

Rachel: So, a knowing or intuition, if you like?

Mike: Absolutely.

Rachel: What do you see as the link between spiritual intelligence and employee engagement? Employee engagement is a big topic right now in this world and something that is vitally important. What was the big finding that you came across?

Mike: There is a plethora of research that focuses on the employee, and whether they are spiritually intelligent will factor into how engaged they are. I shifted the focus. I wanted to see if the leader has spiritual intelligence and how that impacts the ability and/or engagement level of the employee.

Almost all the leaders, whatever they called that which they believed in, utilised and embraced the idea of spiritual intelligence.

They might describe their job as a leader as 'serving a purpose greater than themselves' or 'being very self-aware to understand who they are when they lead.' Interestingly, a traumatic episode in their life would often trigger the desire to self-reflect and to become self-aware, helping them define who they were as a leader. I think that too many leaders are still seeking agreement versus understanding. [True SQ takes one beyond that.]

Self-awareness, then, becomes a big part of being spiritually intelligent and being able to engage people's hearts along with their minds.

Rachel: Do you think that SQ can be measured?

Mike: First, I believe that leadership is not received; it is revealed; spiritual intelligence resides in us.

But I did find very specific quantifiers that are related to spiritual intelligence. One is our ability to think about ourselves in the context of the greater environment or world. Another is our ability to find purpose and meaning in every situation.

The active part of that is transcending our situation to see the interconnectedness of all things. And lastly, is our ability to consciously connect with a Being, a source of Divine Presence that is greater than ourselves so as to help us elevate and grow.

These conclusions came from qualitative research surveys and quantitative assessments in which averages and means were measured. Most leaders scored very highly in at least two out of the four of the above factors.

One unanticipated factor impacting employee engagement is that the leaders themselves felt some lack of safety to express themselves in relation to spiritual intelligence. By default, we are acknowledging that we are never going to get our employees to engage at a full level because we're consciously diminishing our own inner voice that needs to be present.

This conversation really brought out the importance of creating cultures in which self-expression is a strong component. To be a leader that is wise and compassionate, one first needs a voice.

Within the Henka paradigm, I realize that "voice" has to do with Heart and how the heart informs the mind. All this comes together as Spiritual Intelligence. It reinforced for me the need of being seen, heard, and valued as being tops for engagement and for growing in a company or organisation.

This is what Mike means when he says,

'Spiritual Intelligence is my boss.'

1. Spiritual intelligence is discovered internally and expressed externally. So, an individual can be and possess high levels of spiritual intelligence and still fail to impact others if he/she does not intentionally act upon and with that intelligence.

2. It can be difficult to measure but easy to feel, as it is a felt experience that purposefully connects with us on an emotional and cognitive level, whether individually or collectively directed.

3. If Spiritual intelligence in a leader is to effectively and positively engage and impact others, we must look at our internal communication differently. We must stop thinking that all communication starts

in the brain and then travels downwards into our body, and then there is a resulting behaviour. Instead, research (HeartMath®) shows that our heart communicates more frequently and faster upwards to our brain and outwards into our body, thus when leaders listen to their heart with their brain, their spiritual intelligence can speak and inspire more effectively than when we rely on our brains alone.

IQ, we know, measures cognitive horsepower. We employ IQ to calculate and solve problems pertaining to logic and data and to *formulate* strategy. We have also explored what emotional intelligence (EQ) is. It is the kind of intelligence that enables us to build and maintain effective relationships, to know our feelings and to choose to regulate our expression of them and to empathize with others.

As you might know by now, I like to keep things simple. I thought Ken O'Donnell (O'Donnell, 1997) kept it straightforward. He says that SQ helps us maintain inner equilibrium, and IQ helps us interact with things like formulas, numbers, and objects. The following factors are suggested by him for determining one's SQ level:

- How much effort, money, time, and thinking must be expended to get the desired outcome?
- How much respect there is between us on both sides.
- How ethically do we conduct our games with others?
- How much regard we have for the dignity of others?
- How calm we manage to stay despite the strain.
- How rational our choices are?
- How steadfast we are under difficult circumstances.
- How quickly we perceive the good in others

In his book *Spiritual Intelligence* (Benedict, 2000), author Steven Benedict outlined the concept of spiritual intelligence as a perspective offering a way to bring together the spiritual and the material, which is ultimately concerned with the well-being of the universe and all who live there.

More frequently, leaders are being described as "spiritually intelligent", and the best businesses are noted as using spiritual intelligence (SQ) to inform decision-making. Jim Collin's "Level Five Leader" (Lesley Edu) is characterized in this way. In his research, Collins discovered that out of 1,435 organisations, 11 stood out above and beyond the others. The leaders of these great companies were described as having "extreme humility," and furthermore, didn't "seek success for their own glory; rather, success is necessary so that the team and organisation can thrive."

These qualities extend beyond IQ and EQ.

The exercise of SQ often involves deep inner searching and questioning. We use SQ to resolve the most difficult issues, to be creative, and to break out of existing parameters of thought. We use SQ to find meaning and value in disappointment. It is the intelligence we employ when the chaos of change threatens to overwhelm us.

Many of the authors observe that we use IQ and EQ to solve problems within boundaries—this marketplace, this relationship, this line of business. We use SQ *to call the boundaries themselves into question* when the old solutions don't work and when issues of morality, ethics, meaning, and purpose come into play. Thus, according to this line of thinking, when a business abandons a practice because it has injurious financial, environmental, or social effects, SQ is often the capability being called upon.

HENKA IMPACT - IT'S ALL ABOUT ENERGY

It's absolutely all about energy.

Yvonne O'Reilly believes, "If you peel it back to the essentials, there is information, and there is energy. Both information and energy flow through relationships. Energy is always flowing through lines of relationships and when the relationships are disconnected, when something gets in the way of relationship flow, both energy and information are stifled. That hurts business, but it hurts people more."

I asked Yvonne why the coaching leadership style is the one that is least used. Isn't the coaching leadership style needed more as we're entering the fourth industrial revolution?

"Well," Yvonne said, "I believe that's because of the context and the system in which managers and leaders are trained and rewarded". "In that context, the system is really focused on quite a different approach which is often about 'instructing' and 'telling' - what we call top-down command. This command-and-control model of leadership is sadly what most aspiring and up-and-coming leaders have been exposed to and is absolutely not akin to a coaching relationship."

"So partly the reason why it's the least used is that the managers are less skilled in that approach and less comfortable (because they are less skilled). Unless they have a personality that easily has them engage with people and they've had the experience of the transformative output of a coaching conversation as opposed to an instructional conversation. I think it's very hard for a lot of leaders to build that muscle."

"The other reason is, of course, the constant pressure to deliver. Managers are under increasing pressure to deliver bigger, better, and faster - often with fewer resources. The pressure is so intense that perhaps managers and leaders don't think they have time to set up a coaching relationship. The irony is that the organisation is gearing up for long-term pain when the focus is on short-term gain!"

What Yvonne was talking about is endemic pain causing breakages in the system, which is causing people to disconnect and disengage. This is also instrumental in the increased burnout rate not just of individuals but of whole teams. Many organisations realize that they must look at things differently. They must find ways and means to give voice to their people and to give them space to bring their ideas to the table.

"The good news, Rachel," Yvonne said with passion, "is that you and I are also in the arena of working with some progressive organisations who are actually pausing to look more closely at how they engage with people. I believe we can engage with people more effectively by using a coaching approach. Coaching conversations accompany people in richer thinking and help companies draw on "collective intelligence".

It was time to focus on the elements of coaching that would join engagement with delivering on an organisation's goals. The synthesis promised to bring everything in line with an overarching vision in which the sum would be greater than all its parts.

CHAPTER 7

HeadQ – Open and Energising

If there is one major aspect of my own coaching journey that I would say is the most powerful, it is this.

Psychological safety. Punkt. Point. Full Stop.

You may have heard of it and may have cultivated it. But like many terms in leadership or management theory, psychological safety is often overcomplicated. The power of its raw simplicity is its impact.

Coaching is most effective when the person or group receiving the coaching feels a reliable level of safety. Safety allows them to speak honestly and know they will be treated fairly in the coaching relationship.

The creation of psychological safety is powerful with individuals, teams and even with corporate boards.

The person I had to interview is Shed.

Shed (or Stephen Shedletzky) is one of the world's leading experts on psychological safety. I decided to ask him a few questions.

TRUST, SAFETY AND ETHICS (AND A BIT OF THE AWESOME STEPHEN SHEDLETZKY)

Rachel: The term "safe spaces" has been going on quite a bit. I asked my husband, "Do you know what a safe space is?"
 "Yes, kind of," he said. So how important is creating a safe space Shed?

Shed: I think the answer is, 'It depends because the answer is a human answer and all human answers are dynamic, messy, not black or white. So, for you and me [it might rank in importance] as 11 out of 10 but for someone else, it might be a zero or three out of ten. As I talk about it, I attempt to suspend judgment on those who don't yet know or don't view the importance of creating a safe space, psychological safety, or a speak-up culture. Harvard Professor Amy Edmondson truly put psychological safety on the map with her work. I consider her to be the founding mother of psychological safety. In my work, I explain the relationship between psychological safety and a speak-up culture. When you have the input of psychological safety, you get the output of a speak-up culture.

What I mean by speak-up culture is people feel safe to share their ideas (even if half-baked), concerns (even if unpopular), disagreements (even with senior leaders) and mistakes (knowing it will lead to improvements).

I can think of a time when I shared an idea in an executive meeting and was literally yelled at for the idea being half-baked and shared at what was considered an inappropriate time. Regardless of the merit of that feedback, the fact that I was yelled at was punishment enough. Guess how safe I felt taking the risk of bringing up ideas to this executive team going forward?

Rachel: Interesting.

Shed: Alternatively, an employee sharing an idea with someone more senior can have their idea, their behaviour or their strategic choice respected even if it is less than ideal. The leader might say, "Tell me more; it must be hard for you to share that feedback, though I value your opinion. Please, go on."

A tell-tale sign of a safe space or a speak-up culture is if we disagree well — that we can dissect ideas, not people. It means being able to talk about our mistakes, knowing it will lead to improvements on the other end.

If you are a leader interested in innovation, creating a safe space and a speak-up culture is highly important. If you're interested in creating a very hierarchical top-down, old-fashioned "do as I say because I'm in charge" culture, creating a safe space may not be very important for you at all. In this case, I wish that leader the best of luck, but it probably won't yield much fun for them or their people or breed success in the long run.

Rachel: So, why do people find this so difficult to do?

Shed: Because it has to do with trust, and trust is hard. Compassion is hard. Loving someone is hard. Loving and trusting involve risk. Relationships are hard. How easy is it to be married? How easy is it to have employees? How easy is it to have clients? It's not. It is not easy being in a human relationship. Now add on virtual communication and texting. The only person's tone of voice you hear when someone texts you is your own. That's it.

So, you can send me a text message or an e-mail, and I could read it with the wrong tone. I could think, "how dare she." I might then write one back in "defence", saying ", pardon me?" and you think ", now it's on!"

Perhaps, a better approach would be if I just pick up the phone and I say, "Rachel, I'm assuming this isn't your intention because one of our values in our relationships at this company is that we assume positive intent, so I'm going to assume positive intent. But I need you to know that although maybe it was not your intent, the impact of your e-mail is I now have the desire to be distant from you, and I don't truly want that. Your e-mail made me feel small and angry. I know you, and I value our relationship. I'm assuming you don't want me to feel this way, so can we please have a conversation about that e-mail?"

E-mail, Slack and text messages are particularly good for transactions, but anytime that you go into brainstorming, feedback, or emotions, it is critical to pick up the phone or have a face-to-face conversation, whether it is over video or in person. So, is it difficult to do? Yes. Why? Because we are human, and our only truth is our own perception. As a mentor of mine taught me, Your Truth + My Truth = A Higher Truth. Cultivating safety enables one another to seek and understand others' truth, not just our own.

So, we need to work hard at creating safety. The value of creating a safe space, for me, is to "understand" with as much intimacy and with as much depth as possible –what your truth is, and for me to share mine in kind. The worst that can happen is that our truths are not the same. We might not be able to reconcile it, and the best thing we can do is shift the relationship. I've seen brilliant work done with people who hold opposing policy views.

Of course, this goes for differences in the workplace or beyond--on immigration rights, abortion rights, gun control, LGBTQ2S rights etc. I have seen amazing facilitation of people who are on exact opposites of those spectrums, and with the right environment and safe space, along with the right design of questions and experiences, they're able to see, understand, and even accept the other's point of view. They may not hold the other's view as their own, but they can get to a place where they can see how the other does hold that point of view. They can validate and understand. I think that is pretty darn awesome and worthwhile – society needs a lot more of that right now.

Rachel: Absolutely, What about the upcoming generation—the generation that is known for being behind a screen? How will they be able to create a safe space with this accepted mode of "communication?"

Shed: I've seen research with millennials not wanting to pick up the phone. But you can send a voice note, which is obviously much better than a text in terms of picking up tone of voice. While a lot of socialization still happens online, it is much easier to bully online as well. Because it's a lot easier to say something to someone behind the screen than it is to their face. Which, I think, by the way, should be the standard: if you wouldn't say it to their face, you shouldn't type it.

Again, I'm a fan of phone calls or Zoom, especially when it comes to building relationships, exchanging ideas, sharing emotions, and managing conflict.

While I'm all for human connection – it's the very basis of my work and values--I don't think work has to be in person all the time, or go from nine to five, five days a week. That's typically another hierarchical control piece. I believe the nature of the work should dictate how and where it happens. Some work might require that you be physically present, but a lot of other work can be done remotely. In fact, this has been shown to contribute more balance for the individual at work and generate more inclusive work environments. When it comes to human connection, I think the order of it is: in-person meeting, then video meeting, then phone meeting, then voice note, then text-based messages. Anytime there's any friction, I believe there is opportunity to escalate at least one layer up in that Hierarchy of Connection if you will. Hey, I just think we coined a new term!

Rachel: If executives were listening to this and you were to give them a couple of tips on how you can create a safer space. What might those be?

Shed: One of the greatest ways to create a safe space is to bring genuine curiosity. The gateway to curiosity is asking genuine questions. A great question is: "How are you really doing," as opposed to, "How ya doin? Good, great! Let's get to business."

A big piece of a speak up culture is the ability to provide one another with open and candid feedback. And it is hard to provide a senior leader with feedback, especially critical feedback, because we are still a hierarchical species. As a leader, your whisper is a shout, and everyone is listening. I've discovered that the two components that are essential for a speak-up culture are: Encourage and Reward, and it's a cycle. People must feel as though they are encouraged to and that it is worth the risk to their reputation, relationships, and job to speak up and share an idea, a concern, a disagreement, or a mistake. This is a term called voice calculus, and it was coined by PhDs Ethan Burris and Jim Detert. So, we do the voice calculus. Is it worth the risk? And then, when we do speak up, are we rewarded? And by reward, we don't mean a raise or a promotion. The reward is often an acknowledgement, like, "Thank you, that must have been hard to share", or "We appreciate your input. We didn't implement your idea, but here is why." The reward can be in the form of a more strategic insight that may contribute to their overall effectiveness going forward. And, most importantly, "Thank you for that idea; keep it coming." Recognition -- public or otherwise, and awards -- both intrinsic and extrinsic, also typically encourage people to speak up.

The interesting thing about Encourage and Reward is that the more it happens, the more it ripples, positively or negatively. If people take the risk to speak up and it's rewarded, they go back to their peers and friends and convey that it went well or tell them, "You should do it too!"

I know of a pilot, Ben Berman, who is an aviation safety expert. He said that he had a secret when it came to how to create a safe space. It is not unusual to meet your crew a mere 60 to 90 minutes before take-off, yet you must gel as a high-performing and safe-performing team. Every time he met with his crew before departing on a flight, he would call them into a huddle and say, "I have never flown a perfect flight and today's no exception." Just that little context of: I'm imperfect; I have my blind spots; I need your engagement; I need your truth; if you see something, say something, which is a well-known safety slogan. And when they do, you must reward them because if someone says something and then the captain snaps at you, how likely are you going to speak up again?

Rachel: How do you think the creation of safe space – psychological safety – can help with performance and sustainability—both of which are at the core of our Henka Institute.

Shed: In my work with Rich Diviney—who's the author of the book "The Attributes" and a retired US Navy SEAL of 21 years – he introduced me to this notion of peak performance versus optimal performance. Peak performance is when we are at our peak. This is like a football player who plays on Sunday and designs their entire week so that they can peak on Sunday. But we're not all football players, and though we might have big milestone events that we strive to peak for, that's not our typical day-to-day or week-to-week.

Optimal performance is more likely for all of us. What it means is whatever the situation, we give the best that we can with whatever is available to us. Sometimes that's peak, and sometimes that's just gutting it out. Optimal performance isn't always pretty, but it's real, and it's essential for all individuals and teams. Optimal performance is normal life for all of us who are not, for instance, in pro sports. Optimal performance requires rest, reflection, and recovery. We cannot expect sustainable performance to peak all the time – that's a one-way road to burnout.

So, there is a strong link between sustainable, optimal performance and fostering a psychologically safe space and a speak-up culture. When we have a speak-up culture, we have a safe space to share things like, "I'm overwhelmed at home or with my workload" or "I'm caring for a sick family member." Similarly, our leaders can set realistic expectations for what we have to give and when we have to give it.

One example is a winery that knows the team will work their tails off during harvest. It will be harder for them to be present at home, but as soon as the harvest is done, they rotate, and the expectation is to give way more time to family and personal life.

A speak-up culture and a safe space help keep this dialogue real and effective and are essential for designating ways to rest, recover, and reflect, and the expectation to peak all the time is shifted. The alternative? An environment rife with burnout and breakdowns.

Rachel: Absolutely.

Shed: Resilience just means that we can "get through it" and bounce back to our normal functioning. There is actually no growth in resilience, just a return to normal. If we want to grow, we ought to talk about Optimal Performance, which I've also learned from Rich Diviney. Optimal Performance means doing the best we can in the moment, whatever our "best" looks like in that moment. Sometimes optimal looks like a peak, and other times it looks like gutting it out. Sometimes our optimal, all we have, may be ugly, but we're giving the best we have at that moment. In order to perform optimally, we must incorporate rest and reflection, which is key for our continued growth.

Nelson Mandela—who I think we can all agree was a good leader – was asked how he became such a great leader. He said he learned how to lead from his father. His father was a community leader and a chief, and Nelson often followed his dad on his visits to other communities for meetings. He observed his father doing the same two things at all of these meetings:

His father always spoke last, allowing others to share their opinions first. Saving your opinion for last is smart and strategic because by the time it's your turn to speak, you have the benefit of hearing everyone's perspective before offering your own. I've seen senior leaders saying, "Alright, everyone, here's the problem. I need your input; I need your ideas. Here's what I think." No, no, no! You've just put everyone into groupthink-- "Sounds good, boss, let's do your idea!" Remember, as a leader, your whisper is a shout, and it's hard to call the boss's idea bad. When leaders speak last, they gain from the voice and input of others.

The second thing Nelson Mandela observed from his father was every single meeting; he insisted that all participants sit in a circle. There is no apex in a circle. So, another way leaders can design a safer space and set the stage for greater psychological safety is to sit in a circle because it symbolizes that everyone's voice matters.

There is no leader or apex in a circle; it's inviting and safe.

And so concluded this enriching conversation with Shed, with insight, energy, and wisdom in our own safe space.

I thought I'd share some ways for you, as Leader as Coach, to create a safe space while coaching a member of your team:

• Before the coaching begins, establish the intent and focus of the coaching, your expectations for their participation, and your goals for the coaching.

• Ask them what their expectations are for the coaching and what you can do to make it work for them.

• Set the ground rules for your coaching sessions, including how long you will coach, how long your coaching meetings will be if they will have action items resulting from each coaching meeting, and any boundaries for the coaching relationship (such as proscribed times and ways that you are available).

• Maintain a sense of professionalism in a coaching meeting. Do not have side discussions about other aspects of your work together. You are there to create focus and establish a space of motivation, support, and encouragement for them to move forward.

• Make sure your feedback is constructive and productive. Ask periodically for their feedback on how the coaching is going for them. (Even a manager who is primarily focused on execution can keep the inquiry—feedback loop going.)

• Acknowledge their progress when warranted.

It is a delicate balance to be both a person's manager and coach, where you aim to develop a safe coaching space. You can always incorporate coaching tools and techniques in your managing. However, when you enter a coaching relationship with a team member, you enter another territory and must define it. It deserves some critical thinking on your part, and you may need to indicate when you are wearing which hat.

Another consideration involves the purpose of the coaching. Coaching intended to correct deficiencies and improve performance at a basic level is different than coaching to build skills or assist a team member in moving up in the organisation. For some coaching, you may not be able to establish a completely safe space. Think about what safety you can and cannot offer, depending on the individual situation.

When safety is in place, coaching can be a powerful tool in helping managers and their teams excel and perform sustainably.

Here are some ways for the Leader as Coach to create a safe space while coaching a member of your team:

• Before the coaching begins, establish the intent and focus of the coaching, your expectations for their participation, and your goals for the coaching.

• Ask them what their expectations are for the coaching and what you can do to make it work for them.

• Set the ground rules for your coaching sessions, including how long you will coach, how long your coaching meetings will be if they will have action items resulting from each coaching meeting, and any boundaries for the coaching relationship (such as proscribed times and ways that you are available).

• Maintain a sense of professionalism in a coaching meeting. Do not have side discussions about other aspects of your work together. You are there to create focus and establish a space of motivation, support, and encouragement for them to move forward.

• Make sure your feedback is constructive and productive. Ask periodically for their feedback on how the coaching is going for them. (Even a manager who is primarily focused on execution can keep the inquiry—feedback loop going.)

• Acknowledge their progress when warranted.

It is a delicate balance to be both a person's manager and coach, where you aim to develop a safe coaching space. It deserves some critical thinking on your part, and you may need to indicate when you are wearing which hat. You can always incorporate coaching tools and techniques in your managing. However, when you enter a coaching relationship with a team member, you enter another territory and must define it.

Another consideration involves the purpose of the coaching. Coaching intended to correct deficiencies and improve performance at a basic level is different than coaching to build skills or assist a team member in moving up in the organisation. For some coaching, you may not be able to establish a completely safe space. Think about what safety you can and cannot offer, depending on the individual situation.

When safety is in place, coaching can be a powerful tool in helping managers and their teams excel and perform sustainably.

HEADQ – HEAD INTELLIGENCE

HeadQ – Open and Energising – As Shed says - this is all about being in a positive headspace/energy and suspending judgement, co-creating a path forward with others, supporting others in making trade-offs, and recognising cognitive biases and heuristics in self and others.

Heuristics are mental shortcuts that help people solve problems and make decisions more quickly. These rule-of-thumb tactics reduce decision-making time and enable people to perform without continually pausing to consider their next move.

So how can we suspend our judgement?

SUSPENDING JUDGEMENT

Let's face it – we all judge. Our brains are naturally hardwired to make automatic judgements of the world we live in. It is one of the many ways we, as human beings, interpret our own reality. And you know what? That is perfectly okay. What is not okay, however, is when we accept our biased judgement as universal truth and are ignorant of other perspectives. So, how can we, as leaders, suspend judgement in the everyday workplace?

Suspending judgment is a critical leadership skill all leaders need to develop. When we rely on our own biases of how things should be, we will lose the people we are leading. If left unchecked, we can demoralize and oppress our team members with our ethnocentric point of view. We consequently create a workplace culture that is so toxic it could stifle company growth, prohibit healthy relationships, and suppress the possibility of open and honest communication in the workplace. In order to create healthy and high-functioning teams, we as leaders must stop our biases from getting in the way.

Suspending judgment is a disciplinary skill that requires intentional effort and conscious practice. Here are some things that leaders who coach can consider

1 Acknowledge that we all judge

The first step to suspending judgment at the workplace is to acknowledge that even leaders are not immune to being biased. Just because we are in positions of authority does not mean our perspective is right. Instead, we should acknowledge that other people might have better ideas than our own.

2 Commit to being better

Acknowledging our own biases is not enough – as leaders, we also need to *commit* to suspending biases in the workplace. As leaders, we must practice discipline within ourselves and within the collective group. We must be aware of how we receive information and try our best to approach information objectively. We must encourage our teams to challenge themselves in suspending their own biases by setting the standard. By committing to becoming better, leaders make themselves (and those around them) accountable for creating free-judgemental work environments.

3 Be present and listen

Suspending judgment in the workplace requires leaders to be present and active listeners. When we are in tune with the moment, it becomes easier not to get lost in our own biased thoughts. Being present also allows us to be receptive to ideas that we are hearing for the first time.

Being present allows for much-needed pauses. With these brief moments of reflection, our brains can better process what we think when exposed to new ideas. It allows us to catch ourselves when we are more fixated on our own thoughts than on the thoughts of the person we are speaking with.

When we listen twice more than we speak, it allows us to form meaningful connections with our team members. By being present, we are indirectly telling the person with whom we are communicating that we care and respect their thoughts and ideas. Most importantly, we are showing the other person that they are being seen and heard.

4 Always be learning and asking questions

Continuous learning and question-seeking are important parts of suspending judgment in the workplace. We must desire to understand the perspectives of other people and see how they interpret their reality.

When we become leaders, we are no longer exposed to the details that happen in the day-to-day operations of the business. Therefore, we must become reliant on our team members, who are more specialized and more have a more intimate knowledge of certain aspects of the company. As a result, leaders don't see everything and are subject to blind spots.

A leader's responsibility is to connect the details with the bigger picture. Because we are no longer the experts of a specific part of the company, we should be coaching our team members and empowering them to contribute to solving problems. We should encourage cross-departmental collaboration and make our team members excited to be part of the solution-seeking process. Instead of giving answers to our team members right away, we should be asking more questions. By allowing your team members to work through problems and grow from failure, we create a culture of critical thinking and solutions-driven individuals.

5 Be open to trying new ideas and perspectives that are different

One of the main reasons why we would be closed off to new ideas and perspectives is because of the lack of understanding. When things are alien to us, we might become threatened and, therefore, want to stick to what we know is already comfortable.

When leaders in an Organisation are closed off to new ideas and experiences, everyone in the company suffers. Team members become compliant and stop sharing ideas. People are less engaged at work and stop being collaborative. As a result, companies will find themselves lagging in innovation.

Being open to new ideas and perspectives are ways we, as leaders, can suspend judgement in the workplace. It tells our team members that there is no one way of solving problems, a person with authority might not always have the best answers, and that thoughts and perspectives matter. As a result, we create a team of high-performing and productive teams that are engaged and healthy.

Bringing it all together

Suspending judgment is part of a leader's job in creating healthy workplaces. It requires discipline and intention to make sure we don't fall back on our biased ways of decision-making. We do this by acknowledging our own biases, committing to be better, being present, asking questions, and being open to trying new things. By practising these leadership skills, we create engaged teams that result in better and more innovative ways of solving problems. Truly, leaders play a critical role in suspending judgement in the workplace and creating healthy and vibrant workspaces.

COACHING AND NEUROSCIENCE

The latest research in neuroscience solidly supports coaching for transformation. The brain is not static. The brain generates new neural networks and pathways all the time; it phases out the ones that are no longer useful and strengthens those that are used regularly.

If we can change the way we think, we can change neural pathways in the brain, creating new ways of seeing and interacting with the world. Great coaches (like those at Henka!) use tools and techniques that capitalize on the brain's neuroplasticity and promote habits that reinforce the direction we want to go in.

By exploring "thinking", we can create new feedback loops to change deeply ingrained beliefs that trigger responses that, in turn, trigger feelings that lead to either action or avoidance.

As I went through my own coach training, I decided I wanted to be coached by the best. That would be the above-mentioned Yvonne O'Reilly. Working with Yvonne brought me into deep parts of my psyche, my brain, and my beliefs.

The coaching process with Yvonne allowed me to choose new behaviours, and while I cannot prove beyond doubt that my brain has changed, I can say that formerly difficult practices have now become easy habits.

So, if there are observable effects that coaching can have on the brain and on an individual, what might it do for an organisation?

The ICF global coaching study of 2018 quotes a 529% return on investment for an organisation that adopts a coaching culture (ICF, 2018).

For more insight into organisations, I had to explore Frederic's world.

THE WORLD ACCORDING TO FREDERIC LALOUX

I had written a fair bit about Henka when someone said to me one day, "I presume that some of your ideas were inspired by Frederic LaLoux." I had to admit I did not know who he was.

My apologies to Frederic because, of course, I now know who he is and have read his wonderful book several times. This is, I believe, where core principles meet at the top. I do ponder the deep power of synchronicity between Henka and Teal.

HeadQ is the first part of the Henka Model. This is all about being in a positive head space/energy and suspending judgement, co-creating a path forward with others, supporting others in making trade-offs, and recognising cognitive biases and heuristics in self and others.

"Being human is much more than having the right to be vulnerable. It is also, and probably just as importantly, the real possibility to express at work the multiple dimensions of our creative self." --George Por –

Reinventing Organisations – where talent blooms and our callings are honoured

Seeing how my vision of coaching was already resonating so well with Frederic's, I decided to mine his findings, graft some of his rubric onto the Henka Tree and see what more this could mean for developing HeadQ.

Humanity evolves. And just as the quantum paradigm for science and leadership has replaced older models, our existing models of organisation likely need a rethink. In *Reinventing Organisations,* Frederic shares with us a new generation of organisations that are operating in a more spiritual, meaningful, and productive way.

Frederic's treatment of Evolutionary Human Consciousness spoke to my sense that the coaching world needed to stay abreast of the next stages of evolutionary process for leaders and next-stage organisations to operate well.

Frederic talks about how human organisational models have evolved and why we are on the verge of another paradigm shift. The more awareness we bring to these changes, the more confidently we can step into the next stage of the evolutionary process--bringing our organisations with us.

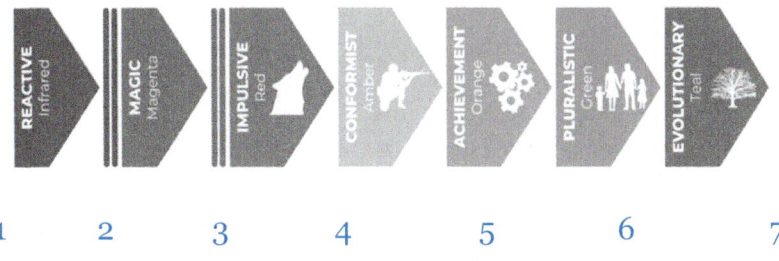

1   2   3   4   5   6   7

Our starting point is indicated by Frederic's succession of the seven major paradigms.

Let's go over history quickly:

1) From foragers without an ego... to
2) bigger tribes with some power... to
3) informal organisations with division of labour, authority, and penalties emerge (but still moblike) ...
4) the transition to agriculture, complete with hierarchies and norms... to
5) individual empowerment and the ability to resist power; the growth of meritocracy... to
6) the emergence of democracy and the emergence of the leader as a servant, where justice and harmony are incorporated into the old success and failure paradigm... to
7) The Evolutionary (Teal) Paradigm, which represents the next step in the evolutionary process and contains a couple of significant game-changers.

One of these game-changers is the speed with which paradigms change. Another is the unprecedented coexistence of people from different paradigms.

We see breakthroughs at this level that solve some major organisational issues. Self-management, for example, is used to run the organisation in this paradigm. Rather than having judgments handed down from the top, decisions are made through conversation with peers. Another feature of this level is that the workplace is viewed as a location where a person can feel complete. This is a shift away from feeling compelled to adopt a professional demeanour at the expense of one's own self. (The necessity to wear masks to secure or preserve one's position in the hierarchy (stage 4 of the evolutionary process) can be removed.) Organisations are viewed as living organisms that develop and evolve (giving for more opportunities to fail and learn), and they are treated as such.

Organisations are viewed as living organisms that develop and adapt (providing for more opportunities to fail and learn) and are part of a larger ecosystem. Teals may align their own objectives within their businesses because they function with a sense of evolutionary purpose. People invest significantly less energy on infighting, ego entanglements, and dealing with bureaucracy when they see themselves as part of this integrative totality, which frees up more creative energy.

Frederic's idea of bringing "all of who they are to work" rather than coming to work as "soulless machines" and the idea of honouring the "Emotional, intuitive and spiritual parts of ourselves" fit right in with the 5 Qs of the Henka Paradigm and its language of wholeness.

This view of the organisation as a living organism entails respect for its wisdom, its beauty, and its evolving consciousness. The Teal Paradigm has adapted coaching to meet this new metaphor. The standard laser attention on senior leaders or to directly address kinks in the system is now made available to whoever is seeking support from an external coach.

It is a great way to encourage an employer to connect with his or her vocation and feel involved. In Silicon Valley and elsewhere, tech start-ups are adopting this practice. [3] Recent research is beginning to demonstrate the importance of moving up the evolutionary model, as researchers have found a direct link between the number of rungs travelled up the developmental ladder and an individual's effectiveness within an organisation. William Torbert, for instance, established that the CEO's developmental stage determined to a significant degree, the success of large-scale corporate transformation programs. Among those, leaders operating from Evolutionary-Teal were found to be by far the most successful.

You will be delighted to know that Frederic and his team operate with a teal mindset – when asking permission (as one has to do in book writing), Frederic's team member was clear that I had full permission (and trust) to write what I wanted. This is the beautiful power of agency.

AGENCY

I first heard the term agency from Noel Fessey. Noel is a fabulous leader who has led both in the armed forces and large asset managers. When Noel first-mentioned agency to me, I thought he was talking about empowerment and cultures of empowerment. He explained the difference to me.

"Empowerment", he said, "is where leaders permit and encourage people to exercise power using individual discretion and a degree of autonomy. But the right to exercise power this way is granted by someone higher in the Organisation. Empowerment – as the name suggests – is conferred. It's a permit. That external quality made me think that it's about utilizing people (albeit with good intentions) rather than human growth. That's why I prefer to think about human agency.

Human agency is innate to all of us. Consciously or not, everyone exercises agency every day to some degree. I believe the role of leaders in Organisations is to maximize human agency for the good of the Organisation and all of its stakeholders. That means helping people to be all they can be – to be the best they can be. Putting it more concretely, human agency is an individual's capacity to make a difference through actions done of their own free will, under effective self-regulation, acting with justifiable self-belief, taking account of the circumstances of the Organisation, and in collaboration with others."

In fact, studies have shown that employees who perceive they have little control over their jobs are nearly twice as likely to develop coronary heart disease as employees with high perceived job control (Bosma, 1997, pp. 558-65)

I conclude that corporate structures are often not yet ready for agency because they live in the Newtonian Paradigm. If an organisation can begin the transformation to a quantum paradigm and sustainable performance, it will operate with a culture of agency. It will begin to innovate and gain a competitive advantage.

Indeed, Neel Raman states, *"Coaching takes a hierarchical organisation and turns it into a vehicle that drives itself with minimal oversight required."* (Raman) Punchline: Leaders need to operate as Leader as Coach.

THE POWER OF SYSTEM 2 THINKING – SLOW DOWN TO SPEED UP

When we think of Head, we might naturally consider the term IQ. When looking at HeadQ, it is worth us looking at the great work of Daniel Kahneman. Daniel is an Israeli American Nobel Prize Winner. In his 2001 book Thinking Fast and Slow, Kahneman talks about fast (system 1) and slow (system 2) thinking. (Kahneman, 2011)

System 1 is quick, intuitive, and emotive, whereas System 2 is slow, deliberate, and rational. Detecting that one thing is farther away than another is an example of System 1 thinking, while parking in a tight spot is an example of System 2. Kahneman's human judgment and decision-making, including all its flaws and heuristics, uses the two-system view as a foundation.

Almost no one is immune to cognitive biases and heuristics when making decisions because of our always-running System 1 and our lethargic System 2. Although most of us identify with System 2, extensive study indicates that System 1 is in command 95% of the time. It is called being human.

It is still up to us to devote time to an analytical approach while making judgments to make fewer errors. That is why it is preferable to think slowly, especially when taking risks or making crucial decisions.

Sometimes, as Steve Hamilton-Clark, Henka's Head of Faculty, often says, "You need to slow down to speed up."

THE POWER OF PERSPECTIVES

Often, slowing down has to do with taking the time to consider another perspective. After all, the view of an organisation as an organism is the realisation that we are each part of a whole rather than the whole story on our own. In our Henka Unlearning Companion, we talk about perspectives (The Henka Institute, 2020)

3 Lenses for Perspective Taking
Considering or assuming the perspective of another is a learned skill. We begin learning it as children --though

young children do this poorly. As adults, it still takes deliberate mental effort as our automatic default is to stay with our own perspective in almost every situation.

In the Henka approach, we learn to look through 3 lenses to gain resilience in moving in and out of a singular view. This is an incredibly useful tool to help coachees make headway in relationship improvement or get a different input to a problem.

Perspective of Self: This is how the situation is understood, or the issue is interpreted from your own experience, based on your own thoughts and feelings in that situation (not to mention one's backstory.

Perspective of Other: This is how the situation is understood, or the issue is interpreted from the experience of the other person involved in the situation, based on their thoughts and feelings (and backstory).

Perspective of Third Party: This is how the situation is understood, or the issue is interpreted by someone who isn't involved in the situation. This is the view of an objective bystander who is looking from a neutral, outside perspective (and their backstory!).

Perspective-taking is NOT the same as what most people think of as empathy. It is not "walking in another's shoes" where the aim is understanding how you would *feel* in someone else's situation. True perspective-taking, which is a skill that coaching can facilitate, is the work of understanding what is going on for others. It is helping another stretch out of myopia that is limiting them.

You can play with this. Try, for example, to stretch and consider:
the perspective of an inanimate object, watching the world drift by,
the perspective of the system,
the perspective of a child,
the perspective of a future self,
the perspective of an obituary writer.

Allow yourself to visit the other end of the pole, sit there for a moment—even while uncomfortable--and then see how that lends perspective. See how that move allows the clenching of one's own position to loosen before gaining an overall wiser, more compassionate view of the whole.

FUTURE SHAPERS/ORGANISATIONAL INFLUENCERS

This is what we have found at Henka:
Relationships and team effectiveness are critical elements of every successful enterprise. Relationships built in the absence of trust and mutual respect become toxic, resulting in inefficiencies.

For a relationship to be built on trust, team members must be reliable, open, honest, and accepting of each other. Having each other's back is an essential element of forming a trusting relationship.

Nothing happens, however, by itself. Purposeful planning and execution by the leader and the team are required every day.

But who sets the tone for this relationship? Ultimately, it is the function of the leader's profile, individual behaviours, and group dynamics. The Leader as Coach is the one that influences behaviours, relationships, and accountability.

Moving away from control and function, the Leader as Coach sets a whole new mood in the organisation. Let us weigh up how the Leader as Coach might differ from the Leader as Manager and the impact this could have on team effectiveness.

HENKA LEADER AS COACH

At the heart of Henka is "Leader as Coach", or leading with a coaching mindset. If anything, the global pandemic moved leaders closer to a coaching mindset.

More than ever before, a shift took place from focusing on the "person" and not the "function". Getting to know and understand personal impacts of the pandemic became a standard item on the Leader's agenda. We asked questions about family members questions about personal resources to cope with isolation and could see (and joked about) the cats and dogs in the background leaping onto the keyboard. By default, we got to genuinely know our team members.

It is tapping into the individual knowledge of a team member that enables us to intersect this knowledge with organisational needs. By engaging on a personal level, you can truly understand and interpret the strengths and weaknesses, the skills and abilities and leverage these for the right projects. It's empowering!

Questions have been raised about whether high performance can be achieved through human-centric and empathetic leadership. Is it possible to achieve collective change, improved accountability, innovative thinking, and increased agility through changing the way we manage relationships? Can it really be that easy?

It is rare for things in life to be easy. Organisations are complex yet simple. Human Beings are complex yet simple. Sustainable Performance is complex yet simple. This is Henka. Like any sport, practice is the key.

CHAPTER 8

HenkaQ –Mindset and Muscle

Henka is like a Martial Art.

Mastering a martial art takes years of training, discipline, and dedication. On average, it takes around eight years to get a Brazilian Jiu-Jitsu/Judo black belt and around five years for a Karate/Taekwondo black belt. Although boxing and Muay Thai don't have belts, I'd say it takes around three years of only one style to master either of the two.

Similarly, becoming a Henka Master requires learning every movement, developing powerful muscles through conscious practice, and harnessing the mind. Only through deep practice, reflection, and feedback on the movements will you become a true master.

In the book *Outliers*, Malcolm Gladwell says it takes roughly ten thousand hours of practice to achieve mastery in any field. There is a lot of debate as to whether this is entirely true. But, as we'll see, it is instructive regardless.

The International Coach Federation also require many hours of training to become an accredited coach, but this is also supported by 100 hours to become an Associate Certified Coach (ACC), 500 hours to become a Professional Certified Coach (PCC) and 2500+ hours to become a Master Certified Coach (MCC).

MUSCLE – THE CRITICAL IMPORTANCE OF CONSCIOUS PRACTICE

Does practice make perfect—or at least experts? In the early 90s, a team of researchers were determined to find out. This group of Berlin psychologists studied the practice habits of those few who reached virtuoso level violin playing. They found that after a certain age, the naturally talented were overtaken by those who put in the hard hours of practice. How many hours? Apparently, a lot.

Malcolm Gladwell has studied the lives of extremely successful people to find out how they achieved success.

"Ten thousand hours is the magic number of greatness," Gladwell said in his 2008 book, *Outliers,* which follows those exceptional people who live on the extreme outer edge of achievement. This became known as the "10,000-hour rule". These studies put holes in the idea that "naturals" float to the top with fewer hours of practice.

We are enthralled with stories such as those about Steve Jobs, Bill Gates, and Paul Allen, who seemingly shot to success through a series of shortcuts. They didn't finish college, right? But what we do know is that Gates and Allen, for example, clocked in thousands of hours of programming practice prior to founding Microsoft. Fuelled with addictive passion, they combined natural ability with practice so that when the time came to launch Microsoft, the two were ready.

The Beatles were a similar story. Initial smaller successes led to an ever-increasing number of gigs until they had played more hours in concert during the time they were an unknown band than most bands play in an entire career. Again, they practised their way to success.

For Love of Practice

No one practices 10,000 hours without loving what they do, at least most of the time. At 13 years old, art prodigy, Akiane Kramarik, was getting up at 5 a.m. to paint and opted for home-schooling to free up additional hours for her work.

Obsession helps. But a strong commitment to practice can advance any endeavour or enterprise. The pandemic brought down many businesses, and the economy will continue to be challenged for the long haul. But still, there are companies that we see thriving despite the crisis. Some have reconfigured themselves and pushed through to more success than ever. Multiple studies show that persistence is the number one quality of success. Anyone who has succeeded in anything can tell you that they have had to overcome multiple obstacles on their way up. So, to rise to the top, we should listen to Jack Benny: How can I get to Carnegie Hall?

Practice, practice, practice

MOVEMENTS – THE HENKA CORE COMPETENCIES

Trevor Hudson and Steve Hamilton-Clark developed several competencies, distilled them, and beautifully defined them for easy access and use. Implementing these competencies not only lays the foundation for individual work but also sets you up to unleash the potential of an organisation. They are:

- Henka Listening
- Powerful Questions
- Get Furiously Curious
- Henka Connect
- Flow, Energy and Range
- Agenda
- Safe space
- I see you

The objective of this book is not to go through each competence, but we do have a wonderful guide to the Henka Competencies which delegates receive when taking part in our programmes.

HENKA MINDSET

A Leader as Coach is about how you "show up". The most extraordinary sportsperson will lose a match if they don't have the right mindset.

In his fabulous TEDx Talk, Dr Alan Watkins (Watkins, 2012) begins by telling a story about Sergio Garcia, the

Spanish golfer, and his inability to overtake Padraig Harrington despite being a superior golfer. Watkins goes on to prove that underlying sustainable performance is behaviour; underneath behaviour is feelings, and below feelings is emotion (or, as he states – energy in motion). Below emotion is our physiology and in particular, our heart rate.

Watkins illustrates that the simple use of breath can regulate the heart rate and have a pronounced impact on performance. Reaching down to the most elemental levels, working with underlying energies, and to align all layers with integrity towards excellence is what good coaching can accomplish. There is no doubt that coaching can be utilised to solve isolated difficulties. Around that, an entire industry exists. However, using it only as a remedial strategy restricts its applicability. Coaching, in both broadening and deepening the conversation -- generating ideas, broadening perspective, fostering connections, maintaining concentration, and igniting passions -- remedies issues but does so much more.

The Henka Leader as Coach will not only need to learn the layer-by-layer Movements that give rise to peak performance but also be able to develop the Mindset that inspires organisations to meet situations optimally and help them actualize their visions.

So that's it.

The Henka Effect.

How Coaching is Transforming Leaders and Organisations.

It just remains for me to offer my conclusion of The Henka Effect.

CHAPTER 10

Conclusion

The Japanese word Henka (変化) means perpetual change, courage, and transcendence

IT is now time for me to conclude this part of an evolving journey of discovery. It has been a privilege to share with you Henka: beautiful, magical, evolving, transforming, and quantum. Henka, as a holistic leadership model with Leader as Coach and Sustainable performance at its core, says to the future, 'bring it on.'

THE IMPORTANCE OF HENKA IN CHANGING TIMES

Keeping my conclusion simple, I'd like to bottom line what this book has covered. It is my sincere hope that the timeless principles and the essentials presented here for effective leadership will make this a book that you will keep for life.

- Our findings show the paradigm is changing, we are deep in industrial era 4.0, and everything we knew, everything we believed, is now under question. Organisations are also changing, and there is a move away from solely profit to purpose. This paradigm is quantum and meets the quantum shifts that are happening all around us.

- At Henka, we believe that human beings have more brains at their disposal than has been conventionally accepted in our culture. That is The Head, the Heart, the Gut (Hunger), as well as a Human Spirit. They inform us more holistically, and we discount any one of them to our great disadvantage.

- If Henka creates an agency, it is your responsibility as a leader that your culture is built around coaching, as described in this book. Even with the best intentions and great skill sets, a leader of an organisation without it is like a boat manufacturer not realising the advent of steam.

- One of the outstanding goals of any organisation must be that performance be sustainable.

- The world and organisations are changing at an exponential rate. Transformation is a given. It is not discreet, and it is ongoing. True Henka territory.

- Leader as Coach is a new critical requirement for this paradigm in supporting the transformation agenda.

If organisations don't recognise the need to transform and embed coaching competencies which both empower the individual and harness the collective, they will not achieve sustainable performance and fold.

My call is to the leaders of organisations to embrace Henka, to be courageous, to stop over-complication, and to recognise that they have the talent inside the organisation to create a coaching culture.

The Henka Effect © Rachel Treece (2022)

ACKNOWLEDGEMENTS

Henka has enabled me to work and connect with some of the most incredible people on this planet. The kindness and support of some of the greatest thought leaders bear testament to the fact that they themselves have moved to a quantum level of consciousness. My acknowledgements and gratitude extend to all those who have supported me on this journey of creativity and growth. If I have missed someone, it is not with intent – it is simply because I am a complex, ambiguous, chaotic human being, just like the world we live in.

First, I must thank my wonderful husband, Keith Dingwall and my daughter Evie who are my World. They both gave me incredible support, encouragement, and love whilst I wrote this book in 2020, 2021 and 2022.

To David White for supporting me in getting me my first proper job. And continuing to support Henka now.

Thank you to Steve Hamilton-Clark for igniting Henka with me in that early coaching session, to Yvonne O'Reilly, who taught me what masterful coaching really is and for your support and belief in true leadership, showing me wisdom and what friendship is. To Marianne

Hermsen, who taught me that it is possible to bridge the spiritual world to the corporate one.

Terence Mauri – you have been the most magnificent supporter of Henka, its philosophy and how it impacts the future of work. Your foreword says it all. Thank you.

To all the Henka team and faculty - it is incredible to see the power of what happens when a global team operates as just that. Every person in the team has been involved in some way, shape or form in supporting me with the book. Special thanks to Lindsey Braik, Helen Barker, Kate Phillips and Simone Peek; your support in the final throes was unwavering.

To the many authors, coaches and thought leaders who have inspired my work through the years Marshall Goldsmith, Michael Neill, Dr Mike Watson, Tony Robbins, Stephen Shedletzky, Mark C Crowley, Jeff Kaplan, Malcolm Gladwell, Daniel Priestly, Dr Kimble Green, Daniel Goleman, Shirzad Chamine, Gregg Braden, Jenna Filipkowski, Hedda Pahlson Moller,and Anji Holland thank you for your inspiration and for inspiring Henka.

To Noel Fessey, Martyn Cuff, Robert McKillop, Ian Holden and leaders from financial services with whom I already feel a lifelong connection and gratitude. Natural leaders as coaches who combine brilliant minds with pure hearts. I am inspired by you and blessed to have found you as industry colleagues and friends championing and supporting my work.

To Verity Ridgman, my first editor—you helped me create structure, simplify, and organize coherently to achieve its intended impact. Your contribution was so important. Thank you to my wonderful subsequent editors, the patient, kind and brilliant Dena Estrin and Luxembourg legend Duncan Roberts who kept me going even when I had other challenges in my life.

To Derek Borthwick – thanks for believing in me and giving me the tips and tricks that are needed for the great publishing journey (which, as you said, does not end with publishing)

To the Board of Henka, Steve Hamilton-Clark, Steve Mele, Chris Howorth, Mark Phillips, and David Micallef, for your conviction, for your belief and for your support and for making this journey a giggle - not everything in life is serious, is it!!

My big acknowledgement must go to the three wise men, Dr Mike Watson, Anthony Smith-Meyer and Michael

May. You are quantum leadership personified. Your kindness, support and encouragement will never be forgotten, and I am so deeply grateful. There were times when I thought this would never conclude – you know what they were.

Kevin Long and Babysteps Publishing. When we talk about trust at Henka, you are trust personified. Working with you has been a joy – I know that you have had my back all the way. I thought that this would be my first and last book. You have ignited the possibility that I could do more. If that isn't Leader as Coach I don't know what is.

To Henka clients and all the Henkees: I admire your own courage in moving to a culture of agency. Your belief in the reset has challenged me to keep thinking creatively.

My vision is that Henka will change lives individually and by transforming how organisations and institutions view and grow people.

Henka has always been about harnessing the collective. This book was not written by me alone. Great things are rarely done alone. It was created by numerous people who have either directly or indirectly contributed to it. Our combined influence is what this work will have on the Planet. We are a part of this wonderful mystery of the developing potential of people. I have a strong conviction that there is yet hope for us as humans in this Cosmos. We haven't even begun to reach our full potential.

Finally, To David Micallef - thank you for being the constant Bernie Taupin to my Elton John. I've always got a great tune, but success only comes with great lyrics. It has only been through your support that Henka is here – living, breathing, and changing our World.

About the Author

The business version

Rachel Treece is the CEO of fts global and The Henka Institute, an Executive Coach, Psychologist, Leadership Trainer, Speaker, Culture and MandA expert.

Previously she worked as an executive within the global financial services sector and has vast experience in leading multicultural environments. She has been working with executives and teams for over 20 years to optimize their performance and create sustainable performance cultures.

Rachel was awarded Most Inspiring Women in Entrepreneurship in 2012 and is a founding member of the Charity Dress for Success (Luxembourg). She lectures at the University of London and mentors young people in various international programmes.

Rachel is a thought leader, speaker, writer, and executive coach and is a leading expert in organisational health, employee engagement, communication, and inclusion. She is a Chartered Marketeer and helps business leaders innovate, adapt, and communicate the age of disruption in which massive yet agile companies are competing for talent

The real version

Rachel Treece is British and, in 2014, became a naturalised Luxembourgish. She is the CEO of fts global and The Henka Institute, an Executive Coach, Psychologist, Keynote Speaker, Leadership Trainer, and Culture and MandA expert.

She is a thought leader, keynote speaker, writer, and executive coach and is a leading expert in organisational health, employee engagement, communication, and inclusion.

Previously she worked as an executive within the global financial services sector and has vast experience in leading multicultural environments. She has been working with executives and teams for over 20 years to optimize their performance and create sustainable performance cultures.

Rachel was awarded Most Inspiring Women in Entrepreneurship in 2012 and is a founding member of the Charity Dress for Success (Luxembourg). She has lectured at many Universities globally and mentors young people in various international programmes.

The real version

Rachel Treece is British and, in 2014, became a naturalised Luxembourger. She speaks four languages and is married to her Scottish husband Keith with a teenage daughter. She lives in Luxembourg but is close to the airport fulfilling her passion for travel (though she did not do much in 2020 and 2021).

The Henka Effect © Rachel Treece (2022)

BIBLIOGRAPHY

Anita Baggio. (2019, October 7). *Anita Baggio Blog.* Retrieved from McKinsey: https://www.mckinsey.com/business-functions/people-and-organizational-performance/our-insights/the-organization-blog/organizations-do-not-change-people-change

Benedict, S. (2000). *Spiritual Intelligence.*

Block, P. (2013). *Stewardship.*

Bosma, H. (1997). Low Job Control and Risk of Coronary Heart Disease. *314 (7080).*

Braden, G. (2015). *Resilience from the Heart: The Power to Thrive in Life's Extremes.* Penguin Random House.

Brown, B. (2010). The Gifts of Imperfection.

Chamine, S. (2012). *Positive Intelligence.* Greenleaf Book Group Press,.

Clarinval, P. (2021). Want To Be A Great Leader? The First Step Is Self-Awareness.

Covey, S. (2004). *The 8th Habit.* Free Press.

Crowley, M. C. (2022). *Lead from the Heart - Transformational Leadership for the 21st Century* (Vol. 2). Hay House.

Dispenza, J. (2019). *Becoming Supernatural.* Hay House Inc.

Douglas, B. (Director). (2019). *The Edge* [Motion Picture].

Frankl, V. (1946). *Mans search for meaning.* Verlag für Jugend und Volk (Austria) Beacon Press (English).

Friedman, M. (1970). A Theoretical Framework for Monetary Analysis.

https://www.journals.uchicago.edu/doi/abs/10.1086/259623.

Friedman, M. (1970). The Social Responsibility of Business is to Increase its Profits.

Gallup. (2016). Employee Recognition: Low Cost, High Impact. *https://www.gallup.com/workplace/236441/employee-recognition-low-cost-high-impact.aspx.*

Gallwey, T. (1974). *The Inner Game of Tennis.* New York: Random House.

Goleman, D. (1995). *Emotional Intelligence.* Bantam Books.

Goleman, D. (1995). *Emotional Intelligence - Why It Can Matter More Than IQ.*

Gosnell, K. (2020). Why every leader should lead at the following.

Greene, D. K. (2012). *The Monarch Method.*

Holland, D. (2015). *Cracking Great Leaders: Liberate Human Energy At Work.* Lulu Publishing Services.

Hurth, V. E. (2018). rganisational Purpose: the Construct and its Antecedents and Consequences. (Working Paper No. 02/2018.).

ICF. (2018). *ICF Global Coaching Study.* International Coach Federation (ICF).

ICF and Human Capital Institute (HCI). (2018). *Building A Coaching Culture for Change Management.* ICF.

International Coach Federation and Human Capital Institute. (2018). *Building a Coaching Culture for Change Management.*

Kahneman, D. (2011). Thinking Fast and Slow.

Kuhn, T. S. (1962). *The Structure of Scientific Revolutions.* University of Chicago Press.

Lakhiani, V. (2020). *The Budda and the Badass.* Rodale Books.

LaLoux, F. (2014). *Reinventing Organizations.* Diateino.

Lattice. (2021). High-Performance Culture: What It Is and How to Create It.

Lesley Edu. (n.d.). The Fundamentals of Level 5 Leadership.

Lipton, B. (2016). *The Biology of Belief: Unleashing the Power of Consciousness, Matter & Miracles.* Hay House Inc.

Marshall, S. (n.d.). https://www.linkedin.com/posts/steve-marshall-0837551_commit-dr-steve-marshall-activity-6728213920093360128-cGaO.

Martin, R. (2022). *A New Way to Think.* Harvard Business Review Press.

McCraty, R. (2015). *Science of the Heart - Exploring the Role of the Heart in Human Performance.* HeartMath Institute.

McKinsey. (2018). Don't stress out: how to build long-term resilience.

Mook, M. N. (2019). Retrieved from https://www.tlnt.com/: https://www.tlnt.com/a-coaching-culture-makes-an-organization-more-adaptable-to-change/

Neill, M. (2013). *The Inside Out Revolution.* London: Hay House UK.

O'Donnell, K. (1997). *Endoquality: The Emotional and Spiritual Dimensions of the Human Being in Organizations".* Editora Casa da Qualidade.

Peele, B. L. (2019). *The Purpose and Profits Roadmap: Making Sense of the Business Roundtable Announcement.* Retrieved August 16, 2020, from http://www.brandonpeele.weebly.com/brt-whitepaper.html

Pips Bunce, J. D. (2022). Retrieved from www.henkainstitute.com: https://www.henkainstitute.com/post/the-power-of-coaching-in-inclusive-leadership

Raman, N. (n.d.). *Transition from Manager to Coach: How to Lead, Motivate and Inspire Others to Maximise Performance* .

Rekhy, R. (2019, November 4). *https://humancapitalonline.com*. Retrieved from https://humancapitalonline.com: https://humancapitalonline.com/learningdevelopment/details/521/leading-from-the-heart

Schaninger, B. (2020). *When one size doesn't fit all: How to make change personal.*

Taylor, F. W. (1911). *The Principles of Scientific Management.* Harper & Brothers.

The Henka Institute. (2020). The Unlearning Companion. The Henka Institute.

Vozza, S. (2020). 5 ways to get better at trusting your gut.

Watkins, D. A. (2012). Retrieved 09 15, 2020, from You Tube: https://www.youtube.com/watch?v=q06YIWCR2Js

Wheatly, D. (2017). Autonomy in Paid Work and Employee Subjective Well-Being. *https://journals.sagepub.com/doi/pdf/10.1177/0730888417697232*.

Williams, F. (2019). The Business Case for Purpose. Friedman, Fink, and the battle for the soul of purpose,. In N. Montgomery, *Building Brands and Businesses for the Twenty-First Century.* New York: Routledge.

Zohar, D. (2016). *The Quantum Leader: A revolution in business thinking a practice.* Amherst, United States: Prometheus.

Printed in Great Britain
by Amazon

10989529R10147